D1256922

COMPUTERS,

COGNITION,

and

WRITING INSTRUCTION

SUNY Series in Computers in Education
Cleborne D. Maddux, Editor

COMPUTERS, COGNITION,

and

WRITING INSTRUCTION

Marjorie Montague

State University of New York Press

LB
1576.7
M66
1990

Published by
State University of New York Press, Albany

Printed in the United States of America

For information, address State University of New York
Press, State University Plaza, Albany, N.Y., 12246

Library of Congress Cataloging-in-Publication Data

Montague, Marjorie, 1945–
      Computers, cognition, and writing instruction / Marjorie Montague.
          p.   cm. — (SUNY series in computers in education)
      Includes bibliographical references.
      ISBN 0-7914-0335-1. — ISBN 0-7914-0336-X (pbk.)
      1. English language—Computer-assisted instruction.   2. English
      language—Composition and exercises—Study and teaching.   3. Word
      processing in education.   I. Title.   II. Series.

LB1576.7.M66   1990
428'.0078—dc20   89-27033
                                                                          CIP

10 9 8 7 6 5 4 3 2 1

To My Son and My Mother

CONTENTS

Acknowledgments   ix

Introduction   xi

1. Philosophical and Theoretical Perspectives   1
    A Historical Overview   2
    Computer Literacy   5
    Philosophical Issues   6
    Cognitive Perspective   9
    Sociological Perspective   15
    Pedagogical Perspective   17
    A Theory of Educational Computing   18
    Writing Process Theory and Educational
        Computing   20

2. The Development of Writing Processes   23
    Models of Composing   24
    Conclusion   37

3. Writing Processes and Computers   39
    Writing Process Instruction   40
    Computer Writing Environment   41
    Word Processing   46
    Writing Process Software   49
    Computer-Assisted Composing Supports   56
    Conclusion   60

4. Computers and Writing at the
        Elementary Level   62
    Writing Research   63
    Computer-Assisted Composing Research   67
    Learning Strategies   72
    Teaching Strategies   76
    Computer Writing Environment   79
    Conclusion   82

5. Computers and Writing at the Secondary Level   83
     Writing Research   85
     Computer-Assisted Composing Research   87
     Learning and Teaching Strategies   91
     Computer Writing Environment   98
     Conclusion   100

6. Computers and Writing with Special
     Needs Students   101
     Learning Disabilities   104
     Physical and Sensory Impairments   111
     Cultural and Linguistic Differences   116
     Summary   118

7. Evaluation and Selection of Computer
     Writing Tools   119
     The Need to Evaluate Computer
       Writing Tools   119
     Considerations for Selecting Computer
       Writing Tools   121
     Instructional Goals   122
     Hardware Selection   124
     Software Selection   128
     Conclusion   137

8. Current Trends and Future Directions   140
     Trends in Educational Computing   141
     Future Hardware   144
     Future Software   145
     Computer Environment for Writing and
       Learning   148
     Professional Preparation Programs   149
     Conclusion   150

Appendix: Computer-Assisted Composing Software   151

Bibliography   175

Index   197

ACKNOWLEDGMENTS

Special thanks are extended to my friends, family, and colleagues who supported and encouraged me during the preparation of this book. I am particularly grateful to Cleborne Maddux, the series editor, who first suggested the idea to me then patiently awaited its fruition. Appreciation also is extended to Susan Craig, who provided excellent critiques of the manuscript, and Lisette Frevola, who assisted with word processing and figure preparation. Finally, thanks are due to Carola Sautter and the editorial staff at the State University of New York Press for their willingness to adjust deadlines and accommodate my needs.

INTRODUCTION

This book has grown from a long-standing interest in and appreciation of writing. As a language arts teacher in the 1970s, I was interested in strategies and techniques to help students improve their writing and, simultaneously, enjoy the writing process. As a learning disabilities specialist in the early 1980s, I focused on the anomalies of children's writing and the difficulties encountered as they wrote. Later, as a university professor, I was introduced to the word processor. This tool not only helped me improve my writing but also inspired me to continue learning about the writing process. Because the word processor substantially changed my life as a writer, it seemed logical that it also could positively affect the writing development of children just beginning to experience and explore writing as a form of self-expression and communication. As tools for writing, computers and word processors have enormous potential for changing the nature of writing instruction in the schools. This book, as part of the computers in education series, advocates computer-assisted composing for children and supports its use in the classroom.

Computers, Cognition, and Writing Instruction focuses primarily on the theoretical implications and practical applications of computer technology for writing instruction. In Chapter One, philosophical, theoretical, and pedagogical concerns regarding the role of technology in the schools are discussed. The importance of establishing a sound theoretical framework integrating cognitive science, computer science, and pedagogical theory as it pertains to computer-assisted composing is emphasized. Chapter Two addresses the nature of the writing process. Using information processing theory as the foundation, composing is presented as an interactive, interdependent set of processes rather than as a series of separate and isolated skills. Several models are described of competent expository and narrative writing that consider both cognitive and metacognitive processes. Writing process instruction and a computer writing environment that encourages and supports the interactive nature of teaching and learning composition skills are discussed in Chapter Three. Various word processing programs and electronic writing tools and computer applications to use within a collaborative, process-oriented instructional model for writing are described.

Chapters Four, Five, and Six focus on writing instruction for elementary, secondary, and special needs students. Presented first in each chapter is a review of relevant research on the development of writing processes and strategies in students. Research in computer-assisted composing is then discussed in light of its potential for mediating writing processes for children and adolescents and influencing their interactions and attitudes toward writing. Learning and teaching strategies for facilitating computer-assisted composing are also discussed.

The evaluation of computer-assisted composing software and hardware is the topic of Chapter Seven. Criteria and guidelines for evaluating computer tools for teaching and learning composition skills are presented and discussed. Finally, Chapter Eight examines several current trends and future directions in the broad field of educational computing and technology. Particular attention is given to the impact of future developments on writing and language arts instruction.

Granted, we are only in the beginning stages of understanding how computers facilitate the development and use of cognitive processes for writing and other academic tasks. It is clear, however, that computers already are an integral part of our culture and will continue to have even greater influence on all aspects of life. The educator's task is great indeed. Keeping abreast of new developments in the field while redesigning the instructional context to accommodate these developments requires considerable time, energy, and commitment. The purpose of this book is to provide educators with an introduction to theoretical and practical issues surrounding the use of computers for writing instruction. I hope that it is both informative and useful. To conclude, I will simply remind the reader that the classroom writing environment must reflect the technological society in which we learn and live. I trust that the educators who read this book will continue to learn, explore, and experiment with the fascinating tools for writing that technology has made possible.

CHAPTER 1

Philosophical and Theoretical
Perspectives

Since computers were first introduced in the 1970s, there has been little doubt that a new age of technology had dawned. The age of technology promised a computer revolution that would dramatically affect the management, storage, and exchange of information and greatly influence the social and economic aspects of society. The business and industrial communities were very receptive to the many ways computers facilitated management, manufacturing, and trade, embracing their use wholeheartedly. The educational community, on the other hand, generally failed to appreciate the potential of the computer as a powerful instructional agent. Although the more curious teachers were eager to try out the computer in their classrooms and eventually realized its capabilities as an instructional tool, most teachers viewed the computer some-what suspiciously, if not fearfully. Many educators felt threat-ened by the very idea of computerized instruction, and some even imagined their replacement by teaching machines! Resistance to change, fear of the unknown, and the threat of having to relinquish authority perhaps are the most significant reasons for teachers' reluctance to welcome computers into their classrooms.

Another source of concern, voiced even by advocates of educational computing, is the potential computers may have for depersonalizing instruction. Ethical issues related to both individuals and society such as loss of freedom, loss of autonomy, and dehumanization are legitimate concerns that need to be addressed as computers become more prevalent in educational settings. Finally, there are issues of instructional efficacy. How does computer-assisted instruction compare with traditional classroom instruction? Will educational software progress at the same momentum as hardware? Will teachers be trained to effectively implement computerized instruction in their classrooms?

Some answers to these questions and concerns already exist. Certainly, fears will dissipate as a new generation of teachers, who have grown up in the computer age, enter the classroom. Efficacy studies already initiated will provide information about the educational costs and benefits of computerized instruction (Culbertson and Cunningham, 1986). Ethical issues may be the last to be resolved, because they require the reflective experience of participants in the technological age. Be that as it may, computers are increasing at a phenomenal rate in schools and homes (Culbertson and Cunningham, 1986). In 1986–1987 there were over 2 million computers in American schools, an increase of 25 percent over the previous year (Goodspeed, 1988). Davies and Shane (1986) predicted that by 1990 more than half the households in the United States would have computers. There is no question that universities and schools must begin to address these issues and keep abreast of the rapidly changing technology and its impact on education.

This chapter will provide a brief historical overview of computers as a backdrop to a discussion of philosophical and pedagogical concerns about educational computing's ever more ubiquitous role in society. Various theoretical perspectives and their influence on the field of educational computing then will be presented to provide a framework for understanding the interrelation between writing process theory and educational computing.

A Historical Overview

Davies and Shane (1986) identified three stages of development in the history of computers. The first stage centered on "mechanical calculator technology" and reached its peak in the mid-nineteenth century. After World War II, the shift from mechanical to electrical systems marked the advent of stage two. During this stage, computer development became increasingly complex and sophisticated, resulting in the introduction of the microchip in 1970. The microchip made possible the storage of huge amounts of information on the chip memory. For example, the contents of the *Encyclopedia Brittanica* can be stored "on a bit of hardware approximately the size of a postage stamp" (p. 3). Stage three, which is currently underway, revolves around the development of optical computers and the use of laser beams instead of electrical current. Because they are not restricted to binary arithmetic programming, these optical computers are faster and more flexible than electrical or microchip models. This new wave of technology makes possible a computer system capable of operating intelligently, essentially replicating the human brain. To illustrate an early development in artificial intelligence, a short story written by a computer was favorably graded by English professors and later published in *Omni* magazine (Davies and Shane, 1986). Over the next twenty years, artificial intelligence will have an enormous impact on education, with expert systems and simulation models for teaching and learning. Computers may become the most effective medium for learning, not only because of the easy access to information through microcomputer networks but also because of their new role as tutor and coach.

In *Beyond the Gutenberg Galaxy*, Eugene Provenzo (1986) claims that the microcomputer has the potential to reshape "not only our social and economic systems but also our traditional approaches to learning, the control of information, and the process of research" (p. ix). His main premise is that our culture has entered a post-typographic era, which has as its center a merger of computers and telecommunications (termed *telematics* by Nora and Minc, 1980).

Telematics presupposes the creation of a society that theoretically has unlimited access to all types of information and data. Stored in databases, with easy access by code, information accumulates and expands continuously over time. In addition to providing databases and information access, these microelectronic network systems also provide for information exchange and other types of communication. To illustrate, national networks such as The Source, CompuServe, or the Dow-Jones News Retrieval Service charge the user a fee for access to their databanks and communicating with other subscribers by sending electronic messages. For access to networks such as these, the user needs a personal computer, a touch-tone phone, a modem for transforming data into acoustical signals, a software communication package that interacts with the network, and a communications interfacing component coordinating the transmission of information to and from other parts of the network (Davies and Shane, 1986). Subscriptions to telecommunication networks range in price from a few hundred to several thousand dollars per year.

The ease and speed of access and exchange of information make these networks indispensable for educational settings. To exemplify how networks can assist in the educational process, Daiute (1985b) begins her book on writing and computers with a scenario depicting how a network can facilitate interaction and communication for teachers and learners. In her example, a teacher receives messages on her computer, provides feedback to student writers, sends mail to other teachers, edits and returns a revised manuscript to her editor, and chats with another subscriber all within a few hours.

The implications of telematics for education perhaps are best understood by examining "the sociology of knowledge." Telematics as a recent but far-reaching societal phenomenon necessitates a shift in the educational paradigm. Concern for the transmission of information will change to concern for coordination and facilitation of information. Functioning within this new paradigm, pedagogy must focus on individualized, student-centered instruction that is cross-disciplinary and disregards traditional, conservative notions regarding the structure of education. Preestablished courses and curricula will be replaced by a curriculum that is fluid, rapidly changing, and geared to the abilities and interests of the learner.

Technological advances in microcomputers continue to occur at a rate reminiscent of Alvin Toffler's (1971) future shock. Indeed, the computer on which I am composing, purchased only a few years ago, is obsolete compared to what is available today at the same cost. How can we possibly expect teachers to stay current with respect to the remarkable pace at which new devices are invented and become available to the public? This concern is tied directly to the issue of computer literacy. What information do teachers need to use computers effectively in their classrooms and what issues surrounding educational computing should be considered?

Computer Literacy

Despite a rather universal acceptance of the position that computer literacy is critical for educators, there has been little agreement regarding the meaning of this term. Defining *computer literacy*, in fact, has been described as one of the most fundamental problems faced by educators. Provenzo (1986) defines *computer literacy* as a multifaceted construct that necessitates providing individuals "with the means to use the computer as a tool in a way that is appropriate to the context in which each person lives and works and to understand the moral, ethical, and social implications underlying the use of computers within the larger culture and society of which each person is a part" (p. 80). Teachers, then, first must be able to teach students how and when to use the computer for access, manipulation, storage, and application of information. They also must be able to anticipate the implications of computers in society and develop in students skills that will enable them to analyze, evaluate, and discuss these implications.

An alternative definition by Culbertson (1986) delineates four categories of literacy: operational literacy, instrumental literacy, literacy as algorithmic reasoning, and literacy as education for altered roles. Operational literacy focuses on the mundane but necessary mechanical aspects of using a computer, such as learning the computer parts, how to turn it on and off, how to boot software, and how to print a document. Instrumental literacy relates more to using the computer as a tool for learning and encompasses skills needed to engage in computer-assisted instruction, including drill and practice, tutorials and simulations, word processing and spreadsheets, and programs to teach course content. Instruction in programming to build students' problem solving and algorithmic reasoning skills is the emphasis of Culbertson's (1986) third literacy category. Finally, role-related literacy alludes to the multiple ways in which computers affect our lives. Role performance as consumers, employees, and responsible citizens is influenced by one's knowledge and understanding of computer technology. Culbertson (1986) goes on to say, however, that computer literacy already may be a misnomer for the kinds of knowledge needed to function effectively in a technological age. He suggests, as do others (Nora and Minc, 1980; Provenzo, 1986), that *telematic literacy* is the more appropriate term to apply to the knowledge and skills needed to deal with the demands created by information and communication networks. In other words, current ideas on what to teach individuals about computers and technology are relatively out of date. As schools continue to debate how students will be taught to operate a computer and use software as tools for learning, skills required for an emergent mode of thinking about microelectronic technologies that is more "futuristic, global, critical, holistic, and goal-oriented in its expressions are already in demand" (Culbertson, 1986, p. 128).

The demands of the technological age require the inclusion of telematic awareness into one's definition of literacy. It is now as essential to know about computers and their place in society as it is to know how to read and write. This expanded definition of literacy involves several philosophical issues alluded to earlier. Although volumes easily could be devoted to the epistemological implications of computers, technology, and information systems for our culture, only a brief overview of these concerns as they relate to educational computing will be provided in this chapter.

Philosophical Issues

Opposing viewpoints are the substance of debate. Since the advent of computers, there has been considerable debate at both the micro and macro levels about the prudence of using technology for instructional purposes. Concerns and questions at the micro level have to do with the impact of computers on children's learning. For example, do computers preclude learning to think critically, as Weizenbaum (1984) proposes or is Papert's (1980) position more accurate? Papert contends that computers help youngsters experience the creation of ideas and knowledge and encourage them to "learn to think articulately about thinking" (p. 27), thus developing their metacognitive as well as cognitive abilities.

Debate at the macro level of analysis involves the effect computers will have on society in general. These discussions have a direct impact on the public's view and acceptance of educational computing. Various caveats have arisen that not only reflect larger societal issues, but are central to the idea of using technology in education. In the previous section on computer literacy, it was mentioned that social, political, and economic issues should be addressed within the context of the total educational program. Students should be encouraged to think critically about the influence computers have on their own lives and the lives of others. As a society committed to individual freedom and democracy, how do we ensure equitable and nondiscriminatory accessibility to computers? How do we involve schools in a telematic revolution without exacerbating racial, sexual, and social inequality (Provenzo, 1986)?

Related to this argument for equal access is the need, according to Broudy (1986), for the reinstatement of general education or "education for citizenship to ensure that students comprehend the significance of modern technology for the public good." Broudy contends that there are various levels of learning in relation to technology. Learning to use technology— that is, skill training—is simply a replicative use of schooling, whereas learning the principles of a technology to solve or invent problems is an applicative use. Two other uses of schooling, the associative and the interpretive, "both use schooling to provide context-building resources of the mind" (p. 250). Broudy's argument that the dialectics of technology requires all citizens to be engaged in general as well as technical studies makes good sense and should help to prevent an elitism that could easily characterize education of the future.

Burns (1984a, p. 200) posits seven questions that should be

addressed if we are to understand the possible consequences that technology may have on the quality of life:

1. Can information technology give more industrial democracy and hence an improved working environment?

2. As citizens, is it possible for us to have any control over which technologies are used and by whom?

3. Will a greater involvement in local and national politics, via "instant referenda," improve democratic decision making?

4. Will individuals have equal access to information?

5. How will information technology impinge upon civil liberties?

6. What will be the effect on our self-image of a heavily computerized society?

7. Will society be more vulnerable and hence unstable with the growth of information technology?

These questions are philosophical in nature and point up the necessity of developing a philosophy of telematic literacy. Several generalizations regarding technology and education can be made based on Burns's questions and his further analysis of the effects of technology on society. That is, education in the technological age must focus on a "whole-life ethic" to ensure equality of opportunity, protection of rights, and equitable distribution of the knowledge and prosperity that technology offers.

Finally, at the heart of these philosophical debates is the rather threatening notion of artificial intelligence. Science fiction, as a mythology of the future, has perpetuated the idea that, if given the opportunity, machines will revolt and take over the world. The personification of machines is an intriguing literary device, one that has inculcated an irrational fear that if we humans are not careful, we may find ourselves in a subordinate, subservient position to machines. Artificial intelligence, where computers are programmed to replicate human activities and processes, plays on this innate fear. An ethic for the age requires a realization of the capabilities of artificial intelligence for understanding human growth and development. This will allow the use of artificial intelligence to enhance rather than inhibit human life.

Research in the area of artificial intelligence, however rudimentary at this time, presents a means of understanding thought processes and brain functions. Michie (1986) claims that computers provide the "acid test" for theory construction. In his view, if a theoretical model has been sufficiently specific, it should be able to be converted into a computer program. As programs become more sophisticated in their construction, what emerges are mathematical models of knowledge and reasoning. The implications of these models for improving the educational process are far-reaching. The development of software incorporating aspects of these theoretical models into their overall design should facilitate instruction in reasoning and problem solving across the curriculum.

Resolution of the disparities of opinion regarding educational computing requires a reconceptualization of the educational process, the curriculum, and the instructional environment. Technology-based education moves the educational process from a linear model to a multifaceted, dynamic, and interactive one. Traditional methodologies and approaches to instruction that organize knowledge in a linear way therefore are not functional within the context of educational computing. An energetic, nonlinear model that integrates a range of positions and perspectives is necessary to encompass practical issues as well as theoretical issues. The following sections will present cognitive, sociological, and pedagogical perspectives currently influencing educational computing theory and the future of technology-based education.

Cognitive Perspective

Artificial intelligence and expert systems exemplify the computer's ability to replicate the human information processing system. In very simple language, this system transforms, reduces, elaborates, stores, retrieves, and uses sensory input

(Swanson, 1987). It has become rare to speak about information processing without alluding to computers either as a model for understanding what humans do when they process sensory information or as a possibility for extending and expanding upon knowledge. For example, Swanson adopts a computer analogy to describe the following three general components of information processing: (1) a constraint or structural component, similar to the computer hardware, that defines the parameters within which information can be processed at a particular stage, such as short-term or long-term memory; (2) a control or strategy component, likened to the software of a computer system, that describes the operations of the various stages; and (3) an executive process, by which learners' strategies are overseen and monitored. Information is sequentially and simultaneously processed or transformed as it flows across the various components of the system. Figure 1.1 represents Swanson's simplified version of this system.

Figure 1.1.
A simplified model of information processing

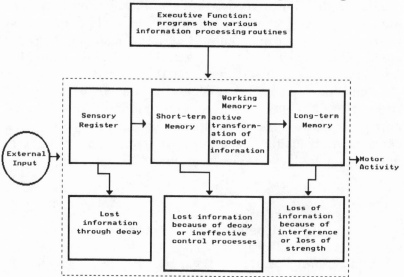

Source: H. L. Swanson, "Information Processing and Learning Disabilities: An Overview," *Journal of Learning Disabilities* 20, no. 1 (1987); 3–8. Reprinted with permission of Pro-Ed.

The blend of cognitive science and computer science has begun to unravel some of the mysteries of human information processing. As an example, John Anderson's (1983) work with the ACT Production System provides insight into the relationships among working memory, declarative memory, and production memory. Figure 1.2 presents his conceptualization of these memory functions within an information processing model. According to Anderson's theory, working memory contains accessible information that can be retrieved from long-term declarative memory, and temporary structures resulting from encoding and production processes. By duplicating these various components through computer simulations, Anderson has further defined the information processing system.

The computer is a natural vehicle not only for a mechanical simulation of human information processing, but also for understanding what has come to be known as the construction of knowledge. Herbert Simon is generally given credit for paving the way for a "philosophy of knowledge in which both members of a man-machine partnership can be allowed to 'know' things, jointly with, and in some cases independently of, each other, or even . . . to create and codify new knowledge for joint use" (Michie, 1986, p. 256). According to Donald Michie, the most effective and least costly way to educate the computer or "get knowledge from a knowledgeable human source, i.e., expert, into a computer" is to let the expert teach the machine by feeding it preclassified examples of expert decisions and then allowing the machine to induce rules or generalize its knowledge. The implications of this human-machine partnership for instructional purposes are enormous. To use writing as an example, it may be possible to "feed" models of writing into the computer, which then produces "machine-synthesized rules" and ultimately is able to conceptually "express" itself. For developing writers, the option would exist for the machine (computer) to become a teacher and branch to instructional programs if rules are broken or to initiate a dialogue with the learner about the mechanical or conceptual problem. For seasoned writers, the human-machine partnership would automatically "self-correct" if rules are broken and converse about the content of the piece.

Michie also discussed what he termed an *integrated*

Figure 1.2.
A general framework for the ACT production system, identifying the major structural components and their interlinking processes

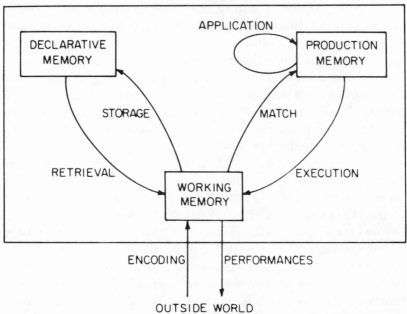

Note: *Encoding* processes deposit information about the outside world into working memory; *performance* processes convert commands in working memory into behavior. These two processes are not central to the ACT theory, unlike the other processes illustrated. The *storage* process can create permanent records in declarative memory of the contents of working memory and can increase the strength of existing records in declarative memory. The *retrieval* process retrieves information from declarative memory. In the *match* process, data in working memory are put into correspondence with the conditions of productions. The *execution* process deposits the actions of matched productions into working memory. The whole process of production matching followed by execution is referred to as *production application*. Note that the arrow called *application* cycles back into the production memory box, reflecting the fact that new productions are learned from studying the history of application of existing productions. Thus, in a basic sense, ACT's theory of procedural learning is one of learning by doing.

Source: J. Anderson, *The Architecture of Cognition* (Cambridge, MA: Harvard University Press, 1983). Reprinted by permission of Harvard University Press.

cognitive system, which would be able to perform a variety of highly complex operations, including forming internal representations of task environments, directing perceptual sampling of the environment to switch execution if necessary, recovering from error states, coping with complex environmental states, working out approaches to goals as they are presented, and relying on past experience to guide future performance. In his view, artificial intelligence and expert systems will enable computers to become coauthors by manipulating and extending knowledge before putting "the knowledge back into human hands in an improved form" (Michie, 1986). Also, an intelligent computing system must have "task-independent capability" much like the human brain's ability to accommodate and adapt to the task at hand. A knowledge engineer's route map (see Figure 1.3), Michie says, can be extended in principle to the synthesis of new knowledge. That is, automation will enable the brain to assimilate and use knowledge that has been synthesized by some other agency (that is, a computer), which is tantamount to enhancing the intellectual capabilities of the human brain!

As futuristic and unattainable as these notions seem, in actuality, technology is advancing toward them at a remarkable pace. The Japanese fifth generation computer project is well on its way to fruition. This "fifth generation system is envisaged as a series of interconnected data-bases and parallel processing machines, accessed by means of an 'intelligent interface machine' which can accept problem statements in natural language, either in typed form or as continuous speech" (Bramer, 1984, p. 149). Figure 1.4 provides a configuration of this fifth generation computer. Instead of simply operating as data managers, the new generation of computers will manage and process "knowledge" while solving complex problems that require reasoning and inference abilities heretofore attributed only to humans (Bramer, 1984). In fact, recently a supercomputer was developed that can solve problems "far faster than scientists believed possible," 1,000 times faster than a normal computer (Rensberger, 1988). "This new 'hypercube massively parallel supercomputer' consists of 1,024 processors—each the microchip equivalent of a single, ordinary computer—linked so

Figure 1.3.
Knowledge engineer's route map

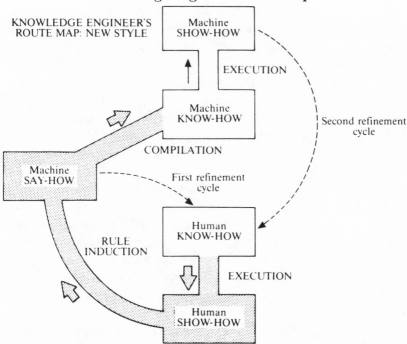

Note: Confirmation is provided by the routine use in the author's laboratory of inductive expert system generators. Under instruction, the expert operates the induction cycle himself, inspecting on the screen, and correcting by applying remedial examples, successive versions of each induced rule. The outer cycle represents feed-back from tests of the rule-base in the field.

Source: Reproduced with permission from *On Machine Intelligence* by Michie published in 1986 by Ellis Horwood Limited, Chichester.

that they work simultaneously, or 'in parallel,' on several parts of one massive problem" (p. 1).

The human-machine partnership is still relatively removed from the sphere of education and the classroom. However, we are embarking on a new generation, albeit a new century, that will transform the typical classroom into a learning laboratory where the teacher, student, and computer work and learn together. As this new approach to education evolves, a sociology of teaching and learning will emerge. This perspective is addressed next.

Figure 1.4.
Basic configuration image of fifth generation systems

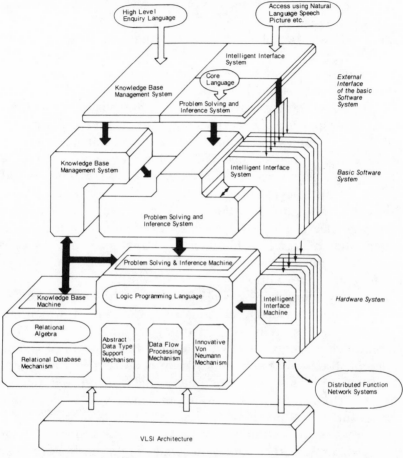

Source: Reproduced with permission from *New Information Technology* by
Burns, published by Ellis Horwood Limited, Chichester, England,
1984.

Sociological Perspective

To ensure the computer's use as a humanizing agent, it is
important to appreciate the new role that technology will play in
all aspects of life ranging from the marketplace to the recreation
center. Burns (1984a) suggests that to incorporate technology
into our postindustrial society and reap its benefits, alternatives

to the work-centered society in which we now live must be found. Essentially, this entails a shift away from work-centeredness to a more social-minded view or whole-life ethic. Only with a commitment to a whole-life ethic, Burns (1984b) says, will we be able to curtail unemployment and its concomitant financial and psychological problems. In addition to its role in understanding cognitive development, technology also will play a vital role in the dissemination of information and knowledge. As the cognitive and moral demands on individuals increase proportionally to the growth of technology (Broudy, 1986), social values will change, and as a consequence, the role of education must change. Education truly will become a lifelong endeavor as individuals increase and extend formal learning time, become reeducated to the demands of the workplace, and engage in learning as a major leisure-time activity. Classroom organization, curriculum design, and educational materials will undergo dramatic change as they continue to reflect the societal changes occurring as a result of the technology revolution.

One of the problems facing education is the information lag in curriculum, methods, and materials. Computers, which are linked to data systems, information exchange services, and communication networks, will alleviate many of the problems inherent in ensuring that information is current and accurate. Providing each child with a computer might be one solution to the problem of information lag in our schools. As Bork (1987) points out, the educational and social benefits of providing a computer for every child may well outweigh the expense, which is only about $1,000 per pupil—a small amount in the total cost of an education. Papert (1980), in *Mindstorms*, decries that educational conservatism has become a "self-perpetuating social phenomenon." However, he sees "a weak link in the vicious circle." He also maintains that

> increasingly, the computers of the very near future will be the private property of individuals, and this will gradually return to the individual the power to determine patterns of education. Education will become more of a private act, and people with good ideas, different ideas, exciting ideas will no longer be faced with a dilemma where they either have to "sell" their ideas to a conservative bureaucracy or shelve them. They will be able to offer them in an open marketplace· directly to

consumers. There will be new opportunities for imagination and originality. There might be a renaissance of thinking about education. (p. 37.)

Fortunately, some educators have begun to think about the impact of technology on education and, ultimately, on society. Indeed, a pedagogical perspective is emerging that necessitates a restructuring and reorganization of the educational system.

Pedagogical Perspective

No longer is there a question about whether computers will be used for instructional purposes. Rather, the question now is how the computer will be used to enhance learning in the schools. If one assumes, as Bork (1987) does, that all decisions as to how to use computers for educational purposes should be made on pedagogical grounds, the interactive aspect of technological education needs to be the focus. The educational community recognizes that learning is greatly enhanced when learners are actively involved in the learning process and given the opportunity for dialogue with teachers and peers. The teaching-learning process, when effective, is highly interactive. However, it is difficult to maintain an interactive learning environment when the number of children in a group exceeds ten (Bork, 1987). Given the present conditions in the schools, it is unlikely that learning will be maximized for all students unless alternatives to current instructional design are found. Computers can provide an interactive learning environment within which students' instructional needs can be met.

For instructional purposes, perhaps one of the easiest and most valuable transitions would be to incorporate word processing into the curriculum. The combination of writing process instruction (Graves, 1983), which emphasizes the recursive nature of the writing experience, and word processing, which allows the writer to engage in the recursive process and plan and revise while writing, makes the student's writing experience more like that of a real writer (Papert, 1980). Application programs, such as word processing, and experimentation with simulations and thoughtware, can enhance the level of cognitive engagement of students by creating a rate of interaction more typical of small group learning (Hawkins and Sheingold, 1986).

The pedagogical strengths of the computer for other curricular areas compared to traditional methods of instruction include more active learning, more varied sensory and conceptual modes, individually tailored learning, learning nearer the speed of thought, abstract learning, and versatility of computer-assisted learning across the types and levels of education (Walker, 1986). Pedagogy, however, must become more sophisticated in its design and implementation and more open to the various ways that computers can continue to enhance and improve the current approaches.

Several other pedagogical concerns were noted by Chaiklin and Lewis (1988) as they evaluated the use of intelligent computer-assisted instructional (ICAI) programs in the schools. As with any other educational innovation, pedagogical uses of computers require a reevaluation of the changing role of the teacher, the subject matter to be taught, the educational goals for the students, the teacher training that might be needed to work in this new setting, and the motivation of the students. Truly, to create a positive learning environment where all students experience success, one must consider the complexities of these pedagogical issues. The various ways that computers can continue to enhance and improve current approaches to education as well as ways to evaluate computer-assisted instruction are the foundation for a theory of educational computing.

A Theory of Educational Computing

A theory of educational computing requires a fundamental conceptualization of the nature of learning. Learning, as a reciprocal process, requires that the learner be challenged by the learning environment and cognitively engaged in the learning activity. As computers become more a part of the educational and learning environment, learners should become more involved and should assume a greater sense of ownership in relation to cognitive as well as affective outcomes (Nix, 1988). The impact of computers on the intellectual and affective development of youngsters should be significant, particularly in regard to how they affect the types and levels of information processing and motivational aspects of learning.

Hawkins and Sheingold (1986) observed several facets of the teaching-learning process they believe to be affected by the incorporation of computers in the classroom. These include curriculum design, learning interactions, classroom management, and the assessment and monitoring of student progress. In their view, the computer shifts the emphasis in education away from learning facts and information toward understanding the structures of information and developing skills in finding, synthesizing, and interpreting information. Additionally, computers provide a creative environment for children to explore their capabilities and further develop their thinking and problem solving abilities. Collaborative learning then becomes the basis of the instructional process. Teachers undergo role shifts to be "less the providers of content-specific knowledge and more the facilitators of students' acquisition of knowledge" (p. 50).

Computers redefine classrooms as "microworlds" (Papert, 1980), which promote "active exploration in an environment that is sufficiently limited and thus conducive to constructive exploration and at the same time rich enough for discovery" (Patterson and Smith, 1986, p. 96). Within these microworlds are numerous uses and applications of the computer: computer-assisted instruction (CAI), networking, creative programming such as LOGO (Papert, 1980) or Handy (Nix, 1988), computer-managed instruction (CMI), computer-assisted composing (CAC), expert systems, artificial intelligence (AI), and intelligent computer-assisted instruction (ICAI). The blend of CAI and AI culminating in ICAI affects instructional technology in a manner that goes well beyond a simple imitation of the traditional instructional approach. The computer is programmed to construct a model of the student's knowledge and processing patterns, which then enables the computer to make cognitive diagnoses of the student's learning, tailor instruction to meet the individual needs of the student, and advise the teacher regarding a student's knowledge levels and progress within the learning domain (Wilkinson and Patterson, 1983, p. 5). These innovations will be discussed further in later chapters as they apply to written composition.

The nature of the educational process should reflect the learning process and all its complexities to better accommodate learning differences and capitalize on developing knowledge. A theory of educational computing is emerging that amalgamates cognitive science, computer science, learning theory, and the technology of learning. McClintock (1988) marks the second frontier in technology and computing as a shift from a culture of memory to one of intelligence, which will require the development of "educational strategies through which people will learn how to control and direct the intelligent tools that will increasingly be available to them" (p. 351). Word processing and composing thoughtware are the products of this second frontier that will transform writing process instruction in the schools. The final section of this chapter addresses the interconnections between writing process theory and educational computing.

Writing Process Theory and Educational Computing

The writing process involves several activities including planning, composing, revising, and editing that are recursive rather than linear in nature and often occur simultaneously. Planning appears to be a central process that interacts at all levels of text production but usually is perceived as being most characteristic of the prewriting period. At this initial point in the writing process, the author selects a topic, generates ideas, and then organizes these ideas into a developing framework. Most writers make notes, develop outlines, or draw representations of their ideas to help them generate words, sentences, and text. Other writers actually revise their plans before they begin to write. Comparing the plan to the written text and then planning content revision before revising is another aspect of planning as part of the writing process. Each activity, important throughout the writing process, can operate independently or in unison with other writing activities as the need arises.

The computer as a writing tool can facilitate the interactive and dynamic nature of the writing process. Daiute (1985b) discussed several ways in which the computer can help by responding to the writer and carrying out the writer's commands. The computer makes writing physically easier to revise and edit, but it also facilitates the planning and generation of text by providing both a sense of audience and what Daiute regards as a minimally social environment.

Writing has been analyzed and discussed within the framework of a variety of theoretical perspectives. Several of the traditional as well as more current theoretical approaches to studying writing are discussed at length in Chapter Two. As way of introduction, much of the work in writing and computing during the 1980s focused primarily on two perspectives, the cognitive and the functional-interactive, both of which provide the foundation for understanding the processes involved in writing and how computers facilitate these processes. The cognitive approach to studying writing is grounded in information processing theory and a view of writing as a problem solving task, whereas the functional-interactive perspective emphasizes the link between the interpersonal context of writing and intrapersonal psychological processes (Goldman and Rueda, 1988). The work of Goldman and Rueda with bilingual exceptional children and that of Levin, Boruta, and Vasconcellos (1983), in their development of the Writer's Assistant word processor program, exemplify this tendency to focus on the cognitive perspective as well as the functional-interactive one and, thus, represent a new direction in writing process research. In computer-assisted writing research, the computer-based writing environment is constructed to provide information on the cognitive processes that children employ during writing in addition to information on the critical environmental and instructional features that promote and support the development of writing in children.

It is important to view writing as a cognitive process, a social process, and a physical process (Daiute, 1985b). With this expanded view of composing, educators can then create microcomputer writing environments that capitalize on these processes and then select the most effective instructional techniques for engaging students in the writing process. The computer enhances the communicative aspect of writing by providing the context for interaction. It also minimizes the need to focus on the mechanical aspects by providing the necessary tools to edit text and eases the physical and cognitive constraints on the writer through information storage, memory search, and idea processing programs. By using the computer as a writing tool, the grammatical and organizational problems that frequently interfere with the writing process can be reduced drastically.

As an aid to problem solving, Patterson and Smith (1986) contend that word processing programs "outstrip just about all other classes of programs" (p. 100). Other types of programs that become natural partners with word processing to help a writer organize and modify textual material include idea or outline processors, dictionaries, thesauruses, spelling checkers, information retrieval systems, text formating programs, and text editing programs. According to Rubin (1983), "by providing tools that facilitate writing and revising, and by creating communication environments that naturally encourage writing, computers may actually be able to offer new opportunities for learning by doing that are not available in noncomputer classrooms" (p. 211). In essence, we are in the midst of an enormous transition in the educational process, one that will affect all aspects of learning and one that will, if managed appropriately, provide the opportunity for all individuals to develop their writing processes and become part of the literate community. The next chapter elaborates on the development of writing processes in children and adolescents by presenting several theoretical perspectives that help to understand the interaction of these processes during composing.

CHAPTER 2

The Development of Writing Processes

The conceptualization of composing has shifted dramatically over the past two decades. Most writing researchers and teachers today view composing as dynamic and process-oriented, a perspective on writing markedly different from the product-oriented view that dominated writing texts and teacher preparation programs in the 1950s and 1960s. This changing perspective on writing produced a myriad of theories and models that seek to explain the cognitive nature of writing and provide a foundation for scientific inquiry. By keeping pace with advances in cognitive science, particularly in relation to information processing models and theories of intelligence, writing researchers have revised their thinking in regard to various aspects and components of the writing process. Most current perspectives place considerable importance on the development of schemata (Anderson, 1978), which appear to facilitate comprehension and learning, and also on metacognition (Brown, 1978), which is associated with the ability to control and regulate cognitive activity.

No longer is writing viewed as a simple, linear activity consisting of several stages that are independent and temporally sequenced. In contrast, writing is now recognized as a complex, integrated set of processes that are interactive and recursive. The prewriting-writing-rewriting model has been replaced by more substantive models that reflect the interdependent nature of thinking and writing. In a review of composing theories,

Faigley et al. (1985) described this departure from the three-stage model of composing as the beginning of second-generation research that characterizes writing as nonlinear and recursive. Although much of what occurs during composing must be inferred from "hard copy" composition or interpreted from writers' reports about their cognitive activities during the act of composing, there is little doubt that writing requires the coordination of multiple cognitive processes. These processes may function separately or in unison and at the conscious or subconscious level, but they always are linked, in some manner, to the goals and subgoals of the writing activity.

The primary purpose of this chapter is to provide a background for understanding the developmental and psychological nature of composing. Composing is a complex, higher-order mental activity that is perhaps best understood within a framework such as the one presented in Figure 2.1. This framework emphasizes the interactions of the cognitive system with both task and contextual variables by representing different cognitive levels and mental processes and the internal and external variables that interact during composing. Several models of competent writing are discussed as they fit within the components of this framework. It is important to note that although conceptual models are limited in their ability to represent the intricacies of psychological processes and the impact of external stimuli on their development and functioning, they do provide a base for understanding the complexity of the cognitive system as well as a clearer picture of the processes involved in writing.

Models of Composing

Writing involves the creation of ideas as well as the ability to express them logically and coherently. Frank Smith, in *Writing and the Writer,* asserts that "writing does more than reflect underlying thought, it liberates and develops it" (1982, p. 33). Thought, language, and writing are related so integrally that it is difficult to discuss writing, much less define it, without using such terms as *cognition, memory, meaning, imagination,*

Figure 2.1.

A cognitive framework for understanding writing processes

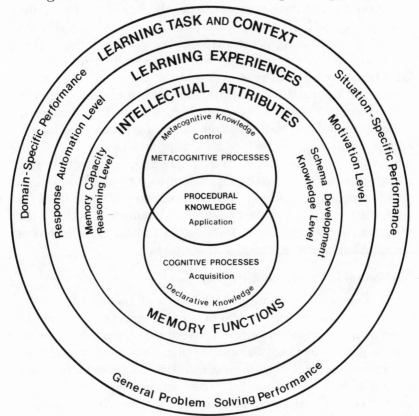

schema, and *knowledge.* The challenge for researchers and theorists is to explain the relationship between thought and writing and also describe the cognitive and metacognitive processes that direct and control writing.

The representation of cognition depicted in Figure 2.1 differs from other frameworks in its interpretation of the hierarchical nature of cognition and problem solving. Concentric rather than linear, it has, at its core, both cognitive and metacognitive processes that interactively process information transmitted via a complex and highly sensitive sensory network. Generic representations of problem solving such as this can be applied across academic tasks that involve comprehension as well as some type of encoding. Writing, as a form of problem solving, will be discussed within this framework.

Several constructs, represented in the intellectual attributes circle of Figure 2.1, are germane to problem solving. Critical to setting goals, making decisions, and reaching solutions, these attributes include a memory system for recalling information, knowledge, and linguistic conventions; conceptual schemata for organizing information and problem data; a variety of general and specific cognitive processes for acquiring declarative knowledge and for planning and executing problem solutions; and a repertoire of metacognitive processes for developing metacognitive knowledge and regulating, controlling, and monitoring cognitive activities. Effective writing is dependent on the smooth interaction of these processes. Viewed from this perspective, writing is visualized as a complex activity that requires the integration of intellectual attributes with various learning experiences, tasks, and contexts.

Intellectual Attributes and Writing

In Figure 2.1, assorted cognitive and metacognitive processes associated with problem solving are depicted by the central, interconnected circles. These psychological processes govern knowledge acquisition, application, and control and determine the declarative, procedural, and executive functions employed in problem solving. They are arranged in the inner circle to imply a hierarchical as well as interactive relationship. Anderson's (1983) ACT theory of cognition provides insight into these knowledge levels and their interactions. Anderson viewed problem solving as the basic mode of cognition and learning as a set of organized, ordered, and goal-structured processes dependent on the interaction of three different memory functions: declarative memory, production memory, and working memory. His primary concern in relation to new learning is the acquisition of declarative and procedural knowledge and transition between the two knowledge types. Declarative knowledge is construed as a network of propositions, which Anderson describes as accumulations of interrelated facts and concepts. Procedural knowledge, on the other hand, is identified as a system of productions or procedures that lead to and facilitate goal attainment. Understanding how these knowledge levels interact and how memory functions operate during writing is a continuing research concern.

The influence of a writer's knowledge levels on writing development has been discussed by Hillocks (1986), who differentiates four major types of knowledge that appear critical to the writing process: declarative knowledge of substance, which essentially constitutes the information or "data" base for writing a piece; procedural knowledge for recalling, ordering, and transforming the substantive data; declarative knowledge of form, which is the knowledge of syntactic, generic, or rhetorical forms and their parts; and procedural knowledge of form or the ability to search for and produce the appropriate form. These knowledge types are related directly to the numerous linguistic and structural conventions that must be adhered to while writing. Once learned, these conventions become part of the writer's knowledge as they link into one or more conceptual schemata. Discourse schemata need not be restricted to certain kinds of information and, indeed, may overlap as the writer searches for concepts, facts, forms, information, or ideas relevant to the writing task. To illustrate, let us consider story schema, the cognitive structure for narratives. This schema is described as a hierarchically and temporally related set of elements generic to narrative forms. The premise of story schema research is that stories contain certain elements that are constructed in a predictable and highly organized manner. Settings, episodes, and resolutions, for example, are characteristic of narrative text. According to Bereiter and Scardamalia (1987), written discourse instantiates the schema "in force at the time" (p. 58). This means that, as individuals compose stories, they produce particular instances of the concepts represented in the conceptual schema. Much of the research in this area has focused on the development of story schemata in young children (Mandler and Johnson, 1977; Stein and Glenn, 1979). Accumulating evidence suggests that, as story schemata develop, they play an increasingly significant role in both comprehension of narrative discourse and beginning writing development (Rentel and King, 1983). As readers and writers mature linguistically and develop knowledge of narrative structure and conventions, their ability to comprehend and produce text improves. Some readers acquire this knowledge naturally as they mature; however, many readers and perhaps all writers require instruction to maximally utilize and coordinate the various processes that interact during narrative text comprehension and expression. It seems clear from the research that many students need to be taught how to gain access to declarative knowledge and also how to appropriately utilize procedural knowledge as they write. "Natural process" instruction, which assumes students will acquire appropriate knowledge and conventions for writing if merely given the chance, usually is not sufficient to produce competent, skilled writers (Hillocks, 1986).

Sternberg (1985) provides additional insight into the intricacies of the cognitive system. According to his theory of information processing, knowledge acquisition and performance components interact with other intrinsic mechanisms known as metacomponents. Metacomponents are defined as higher-order executive processes with a strong impact on learning ability, and these are instrumental in planning, monitoring, and evaluating academic tasks. Writing involves the interaction of the following metacomponential functions: definition of the task, selection of lower-order processes to accomplish the task, formation of a strategy by combining several lower-order processes, formation or selection of a mental representation of the task to act upon, allocation of mental resources to perform the task, monitoring of task performance, and evaluation of task performance (Kolligian and Sternberg, 1987). These metacognitive processes or control functions are used for general monitoring of topic and text organization or for specific monitoring of the technical aspects of writing, such as spelling and punctuation. The importance of metacognition in developing and refining writing skills is well acknowledged in the literature (Bracewell, 1983; Daiute, 1985a; Faigley et al., 1985; Flower and Hayes, 1980; Scardamalia and Bereiter, 1986). Deficits in this part of the cognitive system appear to delay the development of writing processes and impede effective written expression (Kolligian and Sternberg, 1987). Because metacognitive processes are developmental (Flavell, 1985), meaningful instruction can occur only when the learner's cognitive maturity and reasoning ability are at a point of developmental readiness that allows interpretation and adaptation of appropriate learning strategies. According to Faigley and his colleagues (1985), young writers who typically have no strategies for composing extended texts eventually develop general strategies that are useful in all writing situations. A certain level of maturity is required for writers to adapt and tailor strategies specifically to individual writing tasks. Unfortunately, this progression from beginning writer to mature writer usually is not a natural occurrence. Many learners require explicit instruction in managing or monitoring writing processes (Daiute, 1985a).

Using a Piagetian framework, Biggs and Collis (1982) delineated several levels of learning representing the range of intellectual progress from sensori-motor (infancy), through intuitive-preoperation or iconic (early childhood to preschool) and concrete symbolic (childhood to adolescent), to the formal operations of early and mature adulthood. Viewed within this developmental framework, learning is simple and concrete at the beginning stages of intellectual development and becomes progressively more complex and abstract with increasing maturity. By analyzing responses of individuals to various environmental cues within this framework, Biggs and Collis (1982) have constructed a taxonomy, referred to as the *structure of observed learning outcome* or *response* (SOLO). This taxonomy extends earlier conceptualizations of cognitive development by positing a consistent and repetitive structure of levels within hierarchically arranged functioning modes. This view of learning has implications for understanding the development of writing.

According to this interpretation of intellectual development, writing ability can be traced to the movement across different levels as writers acquire and integrate new declarative and procedural knowledge pertaining to written expression. At the extended abstract level, the highest level within each mode, a transition across modes occurs. This transition appears related to the individual's ability to organize and control interactions with the environment (Collis, 1987). Thus, it appears that metacognitive ability is the determining factor that enables writers to adjust accordingly to varying task demands and contexts. Not only is metacognitive ability a requisite for upward movement into more abstract levels and modes, it also is a condition for operating at lower response levels. In other words, metacognition facilitates the selection and allocation of techniques and strategies for successful task completion. Whether metacognitive activity operates at the conscious or subconscious level depends on the nature and complexity of the writing task as well as on the experiential and knowledge base of the writer. Progress through a mode and transition across modes are related to the degree of automaticity and control the writer has achieved in response to varying task elements and operations involved in task completion. Automaticity is an individual's ability to respond to environmental cues or stimuli with little awareness or conscious attending. This response level can be attributed to a combination of maturational factors and relevant learning experiences. As writing processes become more automatic, the writer is freer to consciously attend to more demanding aspects of writing such as style, coherence, and substantive revision.

Learning Experiences and Writing

Learning experiences encompass a multitude of events that, in some manner, alter an individual's cognitive system to produce an observable change in response patterns. Systematic changes over time that are not attributable to maturation are "by definition attributable to experience, and experience in turn plays a role only when learning has taken place" (Tamor and Bond, 1983, p. 106). This explanation may create more confusion than clarification, because experience and maturation, and their respective roles in human development, are neither clear-cut nor well defined. Therefore, it may be difficult to separate maturational learning from experiential learning particularly in an area such as language development where it seems so evident that one cannot occur without the other and where the maturational process is enhanced through stimulating learning experiences. Transactional cognitive models accommodate these relationships by operating from the premise that components are not mutually exclusive and independent, but rather overlapping and interdependent. Furthermore, certain aspects of language development may be more dependent on environmental influences than on maturation. Research tells us that environmental conditions heavily affect the language development of young children (Anderson,

1983; Bloom and Lahey, 1978) and also that children who enter school with well-developed oral language skills generally are better prepared to develop written language than those whose oral language skills are poorly developed (Bereiter and Scardamalia, 1987). Age-appropriate oral language skills, however, may be only one necessary condition for the development of writing skills. Because writing essentially is a school-based activity, it also is necessary to provide an optimal instructional environment to assure that the learner effectively uses acquired oral language skills in developing written language. The relevancy and connections of semantic, syntactic, and pragmatic elements of language to the more academically related language areas of reading and writing must be demonstrated for the learner, and, to go a step further, many skills specific to the writing process must be taught directly if the learner is to develop effective and efficient writing habits.

Learning experiences have a profound effect on an individual's motivation for writing as well as on the level of response to the infinite number of internal and environmental cues that occur during the act of composing. As illustrated in Figure 2.1, response automaticity and motivation are the two major internal states in the learning experiences circle. These internal states interact as a writer develops and influence progress toward proficient writing. In general, the level of response automation refers to the degree of automaticity or control that writers exercise during each facet of writing. Writers exert more or less control over the writing process depending on the level of response automation. The execution of activities such as selecting a word, punctuating a sentence, deciding on the premise of the essay, or editing a manuscript is affected differentially by the degree of automaticity attained for each. Motivation level has to do with the writer's level of participation, the value an individual places on his or her writing, and the confidence and enthusiasm with which writing is approached.

There has been a great deal of speculation regarding automaticity and writing processes and skills, but little actual research specifically addressing this aspect of writing (Bereiter and Scardamalia, 1987). Although controversy exists in the field (Bracewell, 1983), most observers of the writing process conclude that mature writers are capable of operating at the automatic level during all phases of the writing process. There is no doubt that it is beneficial for a writer to have the more technical writing skills such as punctuation, spelling, handwriting, and perhaps even vocabulary selection and sentence production accessible and automatized (Ammon, 1985). Similarly, as metacognitive processes become more automatic during composing, there is less need to exercise deliberate control over the selection and allocation of strategies for written expression. The accomplished writer is flexible and able to reclaim conscious control when automatic responses are ineffective (Biggs and Collis, 1982). To illustrate, goal setting or text deletion may require conscious execution of metacognitive strategies, whereas other procedural components, for instance, monitoring for syntax errors, may operate automatically without conscious decision. Less competent writers may lack the flexibility to move between automatic and conscious control or may have developed a repertoire of inappropriate automatic responses, commonly described as bad writing habits. These writers typically attend more to the mechanics of writing than to the content or level of production. They also seem less able than competent writers to circumvent attentional limitations by employing metacognitive procedures during text production. Examples of metacognitive processes include "planning ahead, reviewing what has already been done, and shifting systematically from one aspect of the emerging text to the next" (Ammon, 1985, p. 77). Several computer-based approaches to facilitate higher-level executive writing processes have been developed. These are discussed in Chapter Three.

Poor writers also may be characterized by low levels of motivation, which are manifested as an inability to actively participate in a writing task or avoidance of writing altogether. The role of motivation in becoming a creative, adaptable writer often is overlooked when studying writing processes. Motivation to write generally is related to an individual's prior learning experiences as well as to the writing task, context, and learning environment. Graves (1984), in a study that compared two different writing environments, concluded that informal environments were more conducive to writing for young children because they give greater choice to the children in terms of what they write, when they write, and how much they write. Tamor and Bond (1983), in their discussion of basic motivational drives associated with the performance of any writing task, suggested that although intrinsic motivation is related to performance, motivation, by and large, is influenced most by outcome expectations. Writers may look to readers for approbation, may wish to please teachers or parents, or may write to avoid punishment for nonperformance. Variation in level and source of motivation affects performance under even the most optimal writing conditions.

Tasks and Contexts for Writing

The writing task and the context for writing also are important in the development of composition skills. The interaction of writing task and context with various cognitive and metacognitive processes involved in the writing process is by no means simple to conceptualize. What must be remembered is that no component of the theoretical model operates independently, and aspects of all components are necessarily integrated into a discussion of any one of the components. With this in mind, the reader will not be surprised that the discussion of learning task and context seems to lead back to the processes associated with cognition and problem solving.

Learning task and context affect three different types of performance: domain-specific performance, situation-specific performance, and general problem-solving performance. An individual's performance is influenced substantially by variations in task and context. Performance is domain-specific, although many of the processes utilized are frequently generic and applicable across several domains. Examples of domains are music, mathematics, and literature. Performance also is situation-specific. Situations can be defined in regard to their environmental and social contexts. Finally, performance is influenced by an individual's general problem-solving ability.

The differential effects of task and context on learning and behavior affect the relationship between the learner and the environment. Sternberg's (1985) contextual subtheory is based on the premise that relationships change as a function of the learning experience and context. His contextual processes of adaptation, shaping, and selection provide the opportunity to adapt to, alter, or select a new environment if there is a mismatch between the environment and an individual's needs, interests, and motives. This three-stage process involves an initial effort to adapt to an environment. If adaptation is unsuccessful, the next step is shaping or changing the environment to meet one's needs. Finally, if environmental shaping fails, the present environment must be rejected and a search initiated for one more conducive to one's interests, abilities, or values. Nurturing environments that facilitate adaptation or that can be shaped easily according to the needs of the individual are required for maximal development. Creating instructional environments for children that will augment the development of writing processes and the acquisition of writing skills is a critical challenge for educators.

Faigley and colleagues (1985) consider writing a social-communicative act, requiring a relationship between the writer and reader. This relationship is affected not only by the environmental conditions, but also by constraints at the knowledge, structural, and rhetorical levels of writing (Collins and Gentner, 1980; Flower and Hayes, 1980). Several aspects of the "rhetorical situation" (Faigley et al., 1985) that could affect the writing process as well as the product include a writer's notion of the audience, the persona or image the writer wishes to project, and the information to be conveyed. Writers must specify their intentions and identify the audience for which the piece is intended. Writing is an act in which the ability to "juggle a large number of constraints" is important (Flower and Hayes, 1980). Competent writers rely on general problem-solving ability to coordinate the multiplicity of cognitive, contextual, and task-related constraints.

General problem-solving performance greatly influences effective written communication. Problem-solving activities for composition include identifying a purpose, setting goals, planning what to say, and then following through on the task. Composing viewed as a problem-solving activity fits well within the rhetorical model of composition pedagogy (Gere, 1986) and the relatively recent cognitive science models of composition (Beaugrande, 1984; Flower and Hayes, 1980). Based on information processing theory, Flower and Hayes' (1980) theory of writing explicates the strategies mature writers use in composition. Figure 2.2 presents a diagram of their theoretical model. By analyzing "think-aloud" protocols of writers who reported their thought processes while composing, Hayes and Flower (1983) were able to make inferences about the nature of cognition and problem solving during the writing process.

Writing processes, according to their model, are organized around the task environment or external conditions and variables, a long-term memory consisting of multiple knowledge systems, and the major thinking processes, which are identified as planning, translating, reviewing, and monitoring. Planning refers to the generation and organization of ideas as well as to setting goals and deciding on strategies to reach the goals. Translating is the actual production of prose, whereas reviewing requires that the writer evaluate and, if need be, revise what has been written. Monitoring, synonymous with the metacognitive processes of regulation and control, helps a writer gain access to appropriate writing processes and rotate them. These writing processes by nature are embedded, overlapping, recursive, and goal-directed. Although not all processes are used in each act of

Figure 2.2.
Model of the composing process

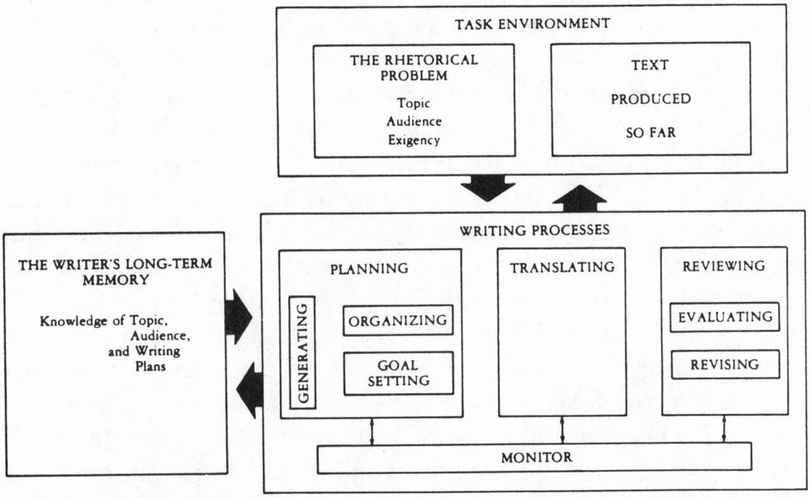

Source: "Writing as Problem Solving": by J. R. Hayes and L. S. Flower, 1980, *Visible Language, 14*, pp. 388–399. Copyright 1980 by Visible Language. Reprinted by permission.

composing, competent writers draw on them as necessary for task-completion.

Other theoretical models of the composition process more closely resemble the artificial intelligence paradigm. This paradigm provides the foundation for research using computer simulations of cognitive activity (Anderson, 1983; Newell and Simon, 1972). Representative of "third-generation" research in composing (Faigley et al., 1985), Beaugrande's (1984) "parallel stage interaction model" of writing processes highlights the influence of sociolinguistics on understanding the development of composition skills. Beaugrande's model, like other interactive cognitive models of writing, emphasizes the simultaneous and recursive nature of writing processes. The difference in this model is its focus on "cognitive" resources that aid writing. These resources of "design criteria," as they are called, include factors such as "noise," time allotment, feedback to the writer, advance knowledge of the task, and novelty within the text. Beaugrande's contention is that each resource operates along a continuum, and the degree to which the resource is utilized depends on the writer's needs at the moment. As soon as a need becomes apparent, a particular cognitive resource dominates the writer's attention and takes control over the writing activity. This model places considerably more importance on the enhancement of cognitive resources than on cognitive strategy use.

Consonant with this viewpoint, Applebee (1986) argued that process-oriented approaches have misconstrued what expert writers do and also have failed to consider how processes might best be taught. He argued for a reconceptualization of writing instruction and a task analysis of changes in teaching methodology that must occur before process instruction can be successful. His reconceptualization of methodology focuses on "instructional scaffolding," where learning is viewed as a "process of gradual internalization of routines and procedures available to the learner from the social and cultural context in which the learning takes place" (p. 108). Using this model of instruction, the teacher acts as a collaborator or facilitator and provides the necessary support or scaffold to allow the child to solve a problem and complete a task.

Applebee's five principles of instruction are presented here specifically as they pertain to writing tasks. Principles such as these provide the bridge between theory and practice for the researcher and teacher by focusing directly on variables that influence cognition and learning.

1. Student ownership of the learning event that includes contributing to and shaping writing activities that represent real language functions, such as informing, persuading, or story telling.

2. Writing activities that consider the prior knowledge and skills of the student, yet are challenging and amenable to instructional scaffolding.

3. A learning environment that promotes natural interaction of thought and language and assists the student in acquiring new skills, strategies, and approaches to the writing task.

4. Shared responsibility for writing based upon the notion of teachers and students as collaborators.

5. Student control over writing and participation as a partner in problem solving and learning.

Conclusion

This chapter established for the reader a theoretical base for writing that focuses primarily on cognitive processes, experiential factors, and task and contextual variables that interact during composing. Theoretical explanations such as those presented in this chapter are essential for understanding how an individual develops knowledge bases, accesses information, creates ideas, and produces written language. Theory is the foundation for practice. The practitioner, however, is concerned not so much with theory as with applications. Modern technology provides the opportunity for educators to apply theoretical knowledge and replicate research in the classroom. As we enter the information age of the twenty-first century, it is incumbent upon us to accept responsibility for closing the gap between what we know about thinking and learning and what we do in educational settings. The first two chapters of this book dealt with philosophical, theoretical, and pedagogical issues related to educational computing for writing instruction. The remainder of the volume will focus on synthesizing research in this area and presenting practical ideas for using microcomputers for effective writing instruction.

Microcomputer writing environments, although still somewhat experimental, seem promising as an alternative to traditional writing instruction. New approaches that focus on computer-assisted composing may preclude some of the mismatches that occur between the writer and writing environment. Although Applebee (1986) did not specifically mention computers in his discussion of methodology, his suggestions for modifying classroom instruction exemplify underlying principles upon which effective microcomputer learning environments depend. Reconceptualizations of the role of the teacher and the instructional environment are necessary if microcomputer learning environments and computer-assisted composing are to become realities in our schools. Chapters Three through Six focus on specific methodologies and techniques for computer-assisted composing, whereas Chapters Seven and Eight discuss evaluation techniques and future trends.

CHAPTER 3

Writing Processes and Computers

In 1985, the National Council of Teachers of English Committee on Instructional Technology recognized computers as valuable vehicles for teaching the writing process (Thomas, 1985). Prior to this, praise was given to computers primarily for features and computer applications of word processing that make the mechanical aspects of writing such as editing and revision simple, routine operations. There are more sophisticated applications to augment word processing, however. These applications, often dubbed *mind tools,* tend to focus on the cognitive and metacognitive processes involved in composition by helping writers think about, generate, develop, and evaluate ideas. Other computer capabilities such as synthesized speech, computer networks, and desktop publishing also are beginning to have an impact on writing instruction. These tools help young writers develop audience awareness by focusing on communication as the primary purpose for writing.

This chapter first will review writing process instruction. This instructional approach for writing emphasizes the interactive nature of teaching and learning as children develop composition skills. Next, a microcomputer writing environment that encourages and supports computer-assisted composing and the development of writing processes is discussed. The last section describes appropriate microcomputer applications and electronic writing tools to use within a collaborative, process-oriented instructional model for writing.

Writing Process Instruction

A process-based approach to writing instruction for school-aged children is best associated with the research conducted by Donald Graves, Jane Hansen, and their colleagues at the University of New Hampshire (Graves, 1983; Graves and Hansen, 1983) and Lucy Calkins at Columbia University Teachers College (Calkins, 1986). This model of writing instruction seems particularly well suited to computer-assisted composing because it is student-centered, stresses an interactive model of composing, considers the dynamic and recursive nature of the writing process, seeks to understand how children develop as writers, and documents writing development by analyzing the writing processes as well as the products (Graves, 1984).

Perhaps the most salient feature of writing process instruction is the collaboration among students and teachers within the writing community. In this community, students write daily and become actively involved in the process. In addition to actually generating sentences and writing them down, students are given the opportunity to think about their writing, discuss their writing with peers or their teacher, revise their plans or drafts, and read their works to other students. This model is especially conducive to collaborative writing and promotes sharing ideas and expertise among students. Collaborative writing can be an alternative to independent writing within a microcomputer writing environment as students work together to produce a story or essay. The microcomputer's monitor displays what has been written, making writing more visible and, thus, more accessible to students and teachers. Printers conveniently provide neat, typed copies of the work in progress for all members of the group to read and critique. As students read their peers' papers and provide feedback to one another about their writing, they develop evaluative skills as well as a sense of audience. The professional appearance of the paper motivates young writers and makes them proud of their work (MacArthur, 1988).

Graves and Hansen (1983) advocated placing young writers in "authors' chairs" to stimulate their thinking about writing and to provide a way for writers to monitor their work. This technique gives children the opportunity to read their writing while others listen. The listeners later paraphrase what they have heard, ask questions, and provide constructive criticism. Using this feedback, authors check the "retellings" against their original work to determine if they have communicated their ideas and then use this information for any clarification or editing that may be required. Writing environments in which students participate as an "audience community" have increased students' writing performance, attitude toward writing, willingness to communicate in writing, and understanding of audience (Graves, 1983; Heath and Branscombe, 1985).

A microcomputer writing environment may be organized easily using these features of effective writing process instruction. The environmental design will vary according to class size, student characteristics, number and location of computers available to the class, and type and quality of software. Although it is desirable to have several computers available for student use, it is possible nonetheless to develop an environment that supports computer-assisted writing with only one computer for classroom use. Daiute (1985b) suggested that a single computer in a classroom can be used as a learning aid for "action-oriented" writing lessons, class demonstrations, and whole or small group activities. It also can be used to demonstrate planning, drafting, and revision processes as students give ideas to the teacher who types them on the computer keyboard. Projection on a large screen enables whole groups to work together to plan stories or other types of compositions. An alternative is to have students first write individual compositions and upon completion of the their first drafts, use the computer to demonstrate technical editing and content revision. This "dynamic blackboard" for writing also can be transformed into a "dynamic bulletin board" on which teachers and students read and post messages (Daiute, 1985b). These kinds of activities help prepare students for composing within a more fully equipped computer writing environment.

Computer Writing Environment

Wresch (1984a) identified six advantages to computer-assisted composing important for understanding the impact that computers have on writing instruction.

1. Individualized instruction and the teacher's ability to select programs and features most beneficial for the writer.

2. Availability of assistance and instruction about writing when it is requested or needed.

3. Feature analysis, which provides immediate feedback and response to writers about mechanics, style, or organization of their writing.

4. Effective use of students' time especially in regard to revision and rewriting.

5. Accommodation of writing as a fluid and dynamic activity.

6. Freedom to write and compose without penalty.

As mentioned earlier, to build upon these positive features of computer-assisted composition and effectively utilize writing technology in our schools, it is necessary to reconceptualize the teaching-learning process and redesign the instructional setting.

The quality of the computer environment affects young children's cognition and social interaction. An environment that stresses problem solving or programming compared with one that provides only drill and practice on isolated skills has been shown to facilitate both cognitive and metacognitive processes associated with problem solving and improve peer interaction (Clements and Nastasi, 1988; Solomon, 1986). In their analysis of computer software, Patterson and Smith (1986) categorized writing tools as a type of problem-solving aid, representing the highest level in a hierarchy of software for teaching higher-order thinking. These tools can be used separately or as components of simulation or tutorial programs to manipulate ideas and data when solving problems. Examples of current writing tools include word processors, idea processors, dictionaries, calculators, encyclopedias, thesauruses, and data management and analysis systems.

A writing environment that incorporates tools such as these

and stresses process instruction can provide the necessary "scaffold" to assist students in their acquisition and internalization of effective strategies for writing. Applebee (1986) conceptualized scaffolding as a process by which the learner gradually acquires routines and procedures through collaboration and interaction with peers and teachers. This collaboration helps students clarify the problem-solving task and understand the strategies necessary for task completion. A collaborative writing environment that promotes exchange of ideas and views writing from a problem-solving perspective supports children as they develop writing skills.

As teachers and students gain computer experience in an environment intentionally structured around the needs of writers, they will begin to adapt to their multifarious roles as facilitators, collaborators, instructors, models, assistants, respondents, and supporters. Chaiklin and Lewis (1988) observed several changes in the role of the teacher when intelligent computer-assisted instruction was introduced into experimental classrooms. They observed teachers giving some of their tasks to the computer, reorganizing what they taught, adjusting the amount of time spent on different activities, and taking on new tasks, which included servicing hardware and maintaining software. The computer can take much of the responsibility for editing spelling and mechanics, while the teacher concentrates on evaluation and revision processes. A teacher's role also would extend to keyboard instruction advisor and hardware and software evaluator. The teacher needs to create an atmosphere where students can develop a sense of independence and feel a part of the community. As students begin to understand the writing process and learn how to function effectively within a social writing context, their questioning skills, their ability to write with others, and their evaluative skills improve (Bos, 1988). Writing with a microcomputer should become as natural as writing with pen and paper.

The classroom or writing environment needs to be physically arranged to encourage interaction among students, teachers, and computers. Typically, computer laboratories have four or five rows of tables on which computers are located. This design does little to enhance communication and relationships among computer users. Furthermore, this arrangement physically restricts movement, thus limiting the teacher's ability to act as a facilitator and guide for students. It is important that teachers and students be able to move freely within the room. For maximum interaction, there should be enough space between tables and computers for several persons to work together. Occasionally, students may wish to independently practice a new skill, try out a new program, or simply write alone. For these reasons, computer carrels should be included in the classroom design. Figures 3.1 and 3.2 show two variations on structuring a classroom for effective computer writing instruction. Figure 3.1 presents a diagram of a computer laboratory that that has been organized to promote transaction among writers. In contrast, Figure 3.2 is a model of a computer writing environment within the context of a typical classroom.

Levin et al. (1985) explored a "functional" computer writing environment organized around a classroom newspaper and

Figure 3.1.
Computer-assisted composing laboratory

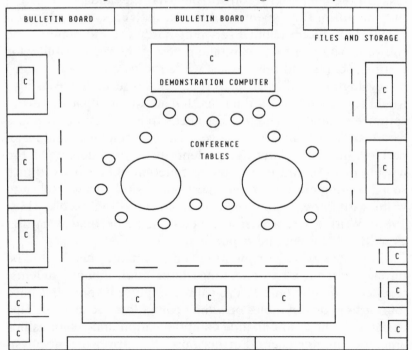

Figure 3.2.
Classroom with computer-assisted composing center

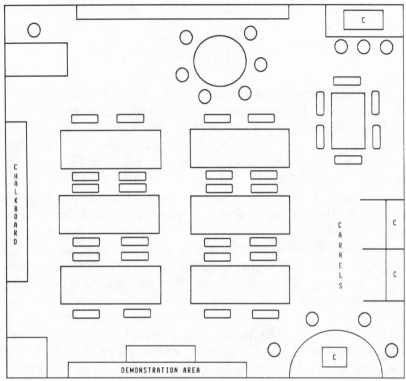

computer text-message network. This environment was modeled after international news wire services that transmit news over long distances. The authors used computer networks to allow students in different schools to communicate with one another and develop an editorial process whereby articles sent via the network were selected by students for editing and inclusion in a classroom newspaper. Although the overall goal of the computer writing environment was to explore unique ways to encourage writing among students, a secondary goal was to develop a social context for writing. These researchers found that within this model elementary students communicated about their own and others' writing, improved their editing skills, and expressed a preference for the word processor over pencil and paper primarily because of its text input and editing capabilities.

Word Processing

Although many attractive features of word processing are cited as advantages, research is only beginning to isolate those with a significant impact on writing development. Beyond the ability to motivate learners, the most frequently identified advantages for using word processors are their editing and revision capabilities, their ability to produce legible copies of text that can be printed on command, and the split screen or window feature, which makes it possible to simultaneously view text and notes.

Perhaps the most intriguing characteristic of word processing is the ease of revision and editing. It is unclear as to how word processing actually affects the amount of revision, as research results have been somewhat mixed and therefore inconclusive (Fitzgerald, 1987). It seems that the type of revisions made by writers differs depending on the instrument used, however. That is, surface revisions (e.g., spelling and mechanics) tend to be associated more with word processing than with pen and paper, whereas content level revisions occur more frequently with conventional methods of writing (Daiute, 1986; Harris, 1985; MacArthur and Graham, 1987). There is general agreement that writers who compose on the computer write more than those who use pen and paper or typewriters (Loheyde, 1984). Quantity of writing, then, appears to increase as a function of word processor use. Although there is some evidence to the contrary, quality of writing also seems to improve as a result of word processor use (Roblyer, Castine, and King, 1988). There is no reason to believe, however, that simply providing youngsters with word processors will be sufficient to maximally develop their writing skills. Rather, good instruction in both writing processes and word processing seems essential.

Other instructional recommendations include teaching keyboard skills in conjunction with word processing commands and encouraging students to develop their own styles of writing with the word processor. Numerous programs with graphics and gamelike features are available for teaching keyboard skills to all age groups. Several of these programs are described in the Appendix. Computer keyboard instruction lends itself to an individualistic approach. By focusing on individual needs, the teacher determines each student's entry level skills and monitors progress over time. Students progress at different rates depending on their dexterity. In addition to the keyboard, other input devices are available. Many word processing programs can be adapted to use a mouse, joystick, light pen, or touch screen. These are excellent options for students who cannot use a keyboard.

Some students may wish to use pen and paper along with word processing for organizing thoughts, developing plans, and making notes. Whereas some writers revise on screen while they compose, others revise only when they finish writing and only from hard copy. Alternative processes associated with content revision and revising strategies should be taught as writers begin to feel comfortable with writing and the word processor. Sommers (1984) noted that word processing contributes to more fluidity in writing, more intensive and sustained revision patterns, more willingness on the part of students to revise text, and a deeper understanding of their writing processes.

The neat appearance of text composed and revised on the word processor is a positive feature of word processing, particularly for individuals who have poor handwriting and whose writing is characterized by frequent mechanical errors (MacArthur, 1988). Writing process instruction stresses the importance of writers sharing their work-in-progress as well as their finished products (Graves, 1983; Van Allen, 1976). It is more gratifying for writers to present a good, legible copy for peer review than a paper with corrections in the margins and between lines. Word processing enables writers to make changes in their writing without damaging its appearance. Young writers are motivated by this capacity of the computer and tend to write more as a result (Daiute, 1985b). However, the "draft" process or reworking a piece until it satisfies the writer and the reviewers must be an integral part of the total writing process. Only then can the piece be "published" and made available to a larger audience. Desktop publishing capabilities of computers, particularly with the introduction of laser printing, enable writers to print professional looking copy that, in many cases, closely resembles typeset material. Writing that culminates in publication makes the writing process more meaningful and gives writers a sense of ownership and control over their writing.

Another advantage of word processing is the window feature. This feature highlights the interactive aspect of word processing by enabling the writer to view outlines, notes, and reminders on different segments of the screen while composing on the rest. Although not all word processing programs incorporate windows, some of the more recent programs do. For example, *II Write,* published by Random House, allows the user to open multiple document windows and rearrange them or cut and paste between them while writing. The window feature is especially important for the writer who works from notes. It can facilitate planning, which is an integral part of the writing process.

There is conflicting evidence regarding the impact that word processing has on planning, however. Similar to the results obtained in computer revision studies, results of planning studies have been somewhat mixed (Haas, 1988). Several studies reported increased planning with the word processor (Collier, 1983; Daiute, 1983), yet others indicated either that word processing inhibits planning or that writers engage in only low-level or word and sentence planning (Bridwell, Sirc, and Brooke, 1985; Haas and Hayes, 1986). One study (Haas, 1988) investigated the differences between how writers plan with word processing as opposed to pen and paper, whether pen and paper supplements word processing for planning purposes, and whether differences exist in planning between experienced and student writers when they use word processing. The results showed less conceptual or content-level planning and more sequential or local word and sentence level planning with word processing for both experienced and student writers. This is not to say, however, that computer writing tools do not hold potential for facilitating information processing during writing. This simply implies a need to identify the most effective instructional techniques for encouraging and reinforcing appropriate planning before and during writing. Haas (1988) suggested that more sophisticated computer-based writing supports may alleviate or diminish some of the problems associated with shaping writers' cognitive processes. These supports are intended to facilitate use of cognitive and metacognitive strategies for writing and may substantially affect the development of writing processes. To distinguish writing support software from word processing programs, we use the term *writing process software.*

Writing Process Software

Three levels of software currently are available to assist writers in developing ideas and analyzing style in addition to the more simple tasks of editing manuscripts for spelling and mechanical errors. At the first level are programs for editing and surface revision. Most word processing packages are equipped to handle these routine operations with optional commands to insert, delete, and copy text or with supplemental software such as a spelling checker or thesaurus. At the second level are more sophisticated writing tools for text and style analysis. Software programs at the third level are designed to assist writers in generating ideas, organizing content, and revising text. These programs exemplify idea processing tools alluded to in Chapter Two.

Level I Writing Tools

Following completion of a first draft, students may use a spelling checker to compare or check words against a dictionary list in the program. This is a valuable tool for many students whose spelling errors interfere with productive writing. Knowing that later they will be able to correct most of their spelling mistakes, students are free to concentrate on content. Possible misspellings of words that do not match or do not appear in the dictionary are identified by the program, which then recommends corrections. More recent programs are also able to identify misused words or homonyms by conducting grammatical analyses to ensure that words are appropriate to the context in which they are used. As an example, the MECC Speller identifies words not found in its dictionary as well as "often confused words such as accept and except." Most programs also have the capability of tailoring the package to meet individual or class needs by adding new words, comments, and definitions to the dictionary. This is an important option because spelling checkers are fallible. There always is the possibility of misidentification or error, especially if the checker contains a limited number of words. Proper nouns and infrequently used words usually need to be inserted in the dictionary or "augmented word list" to preclude their identification as misspellings. Certain programs offer the option of personalized dictionaries. For youngsters who are developing and refining spelling skills, these programs can serve as valuable instructional tools as well. On-line dictionaries and thesauruses have been introduced by several companies to be used by writers for "looking up" definitions or locating synonyms as they write or edit their material. These options are available as part of word processing packages or separately to be used with a particular program.

Level II Writing Tools

In addition to spelling checkers, several programs offer features for checking diction, style, and grammar. The second level of software enables students to critically evaluate their writing stylistic weaknesses. This level of sophistication is exemplified by *Writer's Workbench,* a program developed at Bell Laboratories and later refined for use with students (Kiefer and Smith, 1984). It includes a variety of miniprograms that assist a writer in organizing an essay; evaluating paragraph length; correcting diction by highlighting overused or misused words, cliches, and vague words; and checking spelling, punctuation, usage patterns, and voice. Additionally, this software makes word class counts and summarizes information about sentence opening, length, and type. Quantitative analyses such as the ones offered by *Writer's Workbench* are appropriate for writers who have advanced to a level of writing where style is an important consideration. This type of program helps writers become objective and analytical about their work and enables them to focus on certain weaknesses or flaws before presenting a final draft of their writing to an audience.

Cohen and Lanham's (1984) HOMER and the MECC Writer are similarly designed programs. HOMER conducts quantitative textual analyses for total number of words, sentences, prepositions, state-of-being verbs, certain noun endings, and abstract words. A component of MECC Writer, MECC Editor guides students by questioning them about organization, supporting evidence, style, usage, mechanics, and transitions. Although the aim of these programs is cleaner, smoother prose, the responsibility for revising text lies with the writer. These programs essentially cue the writer to certain attributes of the text, but generally do not provide suggestions about revision procedures. Some programs, such as MasterWrite by Mindscape, have on-line style and grammar manuals to accompany their word processing software. Again, such programs are useful only if students know how to apply the information in the manuals. If writing process instruction is paired with instruction in the application of writing tools, students will acquire writing skills more easily and learn to apply them effectively.

Level III Writing Tools

At the third level, programs and tools are designed to guide students through the various phases of writing. These programs are promising in that they are compatible with writing process instruction by helping writers plan, draft, and revise prose and by reinforcing concepts and strategies taught when using this instructional approach. Usually referred to as *interactive* programs, they originally were developed to assist in the prewriting or planning phase of writing. More recent programs also address composing and content revision. Working in combination with technological aids such as split screens and windows or electronic conferencing for on-line feedback, these programs facilitate and prompt cognitive activity during the composing process.

One popular prewriting program characteristic of this level of writing tools is ThinkTank, which enables students to list and organize ideas and then insert paragraphs within the outline as they develop their essays. Outlining is one technique for organizing ideas and helps writers adhere to a framework or schema for structuring certain types of writing. Production of persuasive or argumentative essays and narratives is assisted with this option. Another computer program developed specifically to enhance prewriting processes uses semantic mapping to develop reading and writing skills. This program, Thinking Networks (Sinatra, 1987), teaches students through an integrated and hierarchically organized curricular package. The program culminates with the introduction of graphic semantic maps to develop skills needed for expository and narrative prose writing.

To specifically guide revising, Daiute (1985a, 1985b) developed an interactive writing process program for school-aged children. This program, CATCH, prompts writers to revise their text and provides analyses to guide their revision efforts. Metacognitive cues and prompts embedded in the program stimulate self-questioning and self-instruction to direct students to evaluate, modify, and improve their writing. Daiute (1985a) stipulated that the CATCH analyses and prompts are intended to link conversation and composition by encouraging children's internal dialogues about their writing and by allowing them enough time to think about textual improvements. Students are placed in control of all evaluations and changes they wish to make. Several features of CATCH offer comments, questions, and pattern analyses for addressing completeness, clarity, cohesiveness, sentence structure, and punctuation of compositions. Question prompts focus on the purpose and content of the piece and encourage students to think about changes before making them. Other options focus on form and offer specific information about word selection and phrase and sentence construction. Daiute (1985a) reported positive effects of this program on the revising patterns of twelve-year-old students.

Several integrated writing programs have been developed to assist writers throughout the writing process. Writer's Helper (Wresch, 1984b), composed of three groups of programs, contains a word processor, nearly a dozen prewriting programs that focus on invention and organization, and several text analysis programs. An example of one of the prewriting programs included to help with writing topic selection is Brainstorms, an automated free-writing activity. This program contains a timer that automatically types x's if students exceed the one-second time limit between keystrokes. If a topic already has been selected, there are programs such as Three Ways of Seeing, a lengthy questioner to encourage further elaboration. The text analysis programs include a homonym checker, outliner, sentence grapher, paragraph development planner, usage checker, and a program to calculate readability level.

Three assumptions about the nature of the writing process underlie the design of WANDAH, another integrated system. WANDAH was developed to help first-year university students in their composition classes (Von Blum and Cohen, 1984). The first assumption underlying the system was the authors' view of composing as a problem-solving task involving words and requiring the integration of disparate cognitive skills. A second assumption had to do with the capability of computers to help students reduce cognitive load characteristic of certain phases of the writing process. The third assumption was the belief that WANDAH could be incorporated into classroom instruction despite the various technological and time constraints it might present. WANDAH was designed around three major components: a powerful yet friendly word processor, a set of prewriting activities to aid in planning and idea generation, and a set of aids to facilitate thematic, stylistic, and grammatical revision. Figure 3.3 provides an overview of WANDAH's features.

WANDAH's prewriting aids, which can be used at any time while writing, include several innovative ideas. One of these, "nutshelling," requires the student to succinctly summarize the purpose, audience, and main ideas of the work and then think about a strategy to attack the writing problem. Another prewriting aid, "invisible writing," asks the student to turn off the screen before writing. This technique purportedly reduces the urge to edit while writing and frees the writer to express ideas and thoughts that might otherwise be inhibited (Marcus, 1983).

Reviewing and revising aids consist of three programs for mechanics, style, and organization of a composition. An interesting approach to revising for style is the "overview summary outline," which presents the writer with two outlining options. If the first option is selected, the student receives an outline of the completed essay composed of the first sentence of each paragraph. The second option requires the student to

Figure 3.3.
WANDAH overview

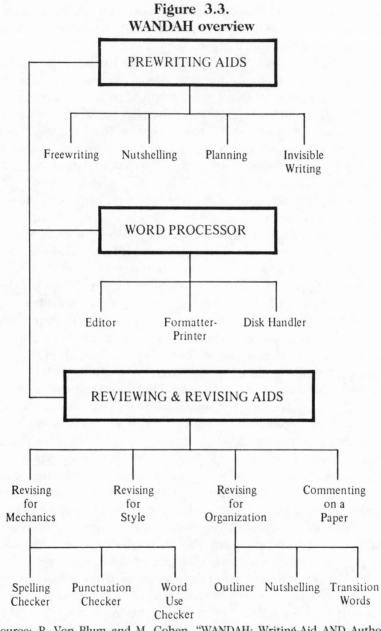

select one "main idea" sentence from each paragraph to complete the outline. Such outlines help students monitor their original ideas by comparing them to their prewriting plans and then evaluating the progression of the essay's ideas. WANDAH also includes a commenting aid, which allows peers and instructors to read one another's papers and make comments that will then appear underlined and in boldface type in the text. These comments can be saved on disk and printed for later review.

DRAFT is another integrated composing program designed to provide conventional text-editing tools as well as facilitate the formulation, organization, and expression of ideas (Neuwirth, 1984). This program, developed at Carnegie-Mellon University, focuses on the following goals:

1. Guide writers during the composing process.

2. Aid instructors in diagnosing problems.

3. Provide students with writing strategies to improve their text.

4. Study the composing processes while implementing the experimental writing program.

5. Provide an electronic composing format and text editor to assist with writing activities.

The program is highly structured and incorporates a systematic approach for developing a composition. Students essentially follow an outline as they create their essay, while having access to any of the technical supports. By using windows, students can simultaneously view different parts of their manuscripts, their notes for writing, and the references. Another useful feature of DRAFT is its comment option, whereby peers and instructors insert comments on a student's paper at any time during its production. The writer then has the option of viewing the comments and accepting or rejecting the advice. This option provides writers with timely feedback and encourages writers to generate and use alternative strategies for solving composition problems.

The final integrated program to be described is QUILL (Rubin, 1983; Rubin and Bruce, 1985). The authors based this program on several "pedagogical goals in the teaching of writing" (Rubin and Bruce, 1985, p. 100), including integrating reading and writing, making writing public, supporting meaningful communication with real audiences, and encouraging writing with and for peers. QUILL is somewhat different from the other integrated programs described in this section in that some functions of its component programs are independent of one another and yet can be used compatibly in an integrated writing process program. One of the component programs helps children with planning and critical thinking, whereas additional programs focus specifically on information exchange or publication of writing. QUILL contains the following six components:

1. Planner, a set of planning aids.

2. Library, an information exchange.

3. Publisher, a set of publication aids.

4. Mailbag, a message system.

5. Story Maker, activity kits for stories.

6. Writer's Assistant, a text editor developed by Levin, Boruta, and Vasconcellos (1983).

Perhaps the greatest strength of these programs is their ability to actively involve children in the writing process. Students work collaboratively to develop plans for essays, exchange messages via Mailbag, and publish their writing for others to read (Rubin and Bruce, 1985). The authors provide a series of lesson plans to guide teachers in setting up a computer writing environment and in implementing QUILL activities.

Computer-Assisted Composing Supports

Several additional computerized supports for writing include genre-based programs, synthesized speech programs, and telecommunication networks. These programs supplement computerized writing process instruction in the classroom either by providing individualized assistance to writers or by encouraging collaboration and sharing among writers.

Genre-based programs emphasize specific types of writing that students are asked to do. An example of this approach to writing is Wordsworth II, originally developed for college students but easily adapted for younger writers (Selfe, 1984). This comprehensive program consists of eight process-based modules to enhance composition instruction in description, narration, classification, evaluation, persuasion, journal writing, comparison and contrast, and critical essays about literature. The modules are divided into planning and polishing programs to assist writers as they plan, compose, and revise their writing. A guide helps the writer focus on the main characteristics of the genre and provides various strategies to facilitate development of the composition. The planning program for narration begins with a review of important parts of a narrative piece such as conflict, character, plot, setting, detail, and resolution. It also includes several branching levels to give students explanations of these elements and practice to enhance their understanding. Thus, a narrative prose assignment becomes more than a writing exercise. Students are engaged in a learning process and acquire a deeper understanding of the genre and the writing process. The polishing program helps students identify strengths and weaknesses of their writing and develop a plan for revision.

Some of the genre-based computer programs have built-in word processors. CAW: Computer Assisted Writing, published by Educational Activities, for example, includes a word processor and focuses on the following three forms of writing: the business letter of complaint, the report, and the persuasive composition. Writing Process Workshop, published by the same company, incorporates an eight-step writing process model and provides word processor templates for persuasive writing, autobiographical incidents, evaluation essays, information reports, analysis, biographical sketches, eyewitness memoirs, and stories.

However, by far the most common genre-based program is the narrative or story writing program. Although creative writing software is available for all age groups, most of the programs have been developed for children in the elementary grades. Story Maker from the QUILL package exemplifies this type of program, wherein children construct stories by choosing options from a set of preestablished story parts. It is the intention of the authors that children become familiar with and internalize the elements of narrative prose. By manipulating large segments of text, children focus on ideas and concepts rather than lower levels of language. Presumably, they develop necessary skills to create text that flows smoothly and logically and also learn to focus on character development and the communication of characters' plans (Rubin, 1983). After making a series of choices from the story tree, the child then has a completed story to read to teachers, peers, or parents. Other story writing programs feature story starters or provide the option to develop personalized story starters. They also provide a story structure to guide the writer through the narrative development. The advantage of genre-based programs is their ability to stimulate children's creativity and self-expression while developing writing processes.

Speech synthesis is yet another technological breakthrough that has enormous implications for teaching youngsters, particularly those with communication disorders, learning disabilities, or other special needs. Computers first produced digitized speech, which involved converting digital numbers to signals that were then sent to a speaker. Recent developments that make speech synthesis more available and much less expensive involve the measurement and transformation of vocal tract characteristics into algorithms to produce speech that sounds more natural than digital speech. With this electronic tool, students are able to listen to text as they produce it or wait to "read through" the piece when they finish writing. This feature permits readers and writers a variety of options. For example, voice synthesis makes error monitoring and correction easier by providing both auditory and visual input to the writer. Voice synthesis also enables youngsters who ordinarily would not be able to read their classmates' writing to do so.

Many programs use speech attachments such as Echo or Cricket as augmentative devices. Talking Screen Textwriter, developed by Rosegrant and Cooper (1983); Dr. Peet's Talk/Writer, published by Hartley Courseware; and KEYTALK by

Peal Software are examples of word processing programs that incorporate voice synthesis attachments. Several studies of "talking word processors" and reading and writing skills have yielded promising results (Kurth and Kurth, 1987; Lehrer et al., 1987; Rosegrant, 1986). Apparently, when provided with the speech option, young children produce longer and higher-quality compositions. Additionally, some evidence suggests that speech synthesis in conjunction with word processing facilitates beginning reading and writing processes (Lehrer et al., 1987).

Telecommunication networks for sending and receiving electronic mail are a third innovation to augment computer-assisted composing programs. Both classroom and long distance computer networks encourage students to communicate with peers and teachers in a supportive and helping environment. Writing conferences are an integral part of writing process instruction and are critical to the development of writing skills (Gere, 1987). As part of the writing environment, telecommunication networks encourage conferences and enhance the development of important writing skills. Using these programs, students begin to critically analyze their own and others' writing, identify writing problems, and solve problems using feedback and input from other students and their teachers. Furthermore, networks provide experience in writing for audiences of different backgrounds, ages, or interests. The most notable advantage of computerized networks over face-to-face conversations is increased opportunity to interact with and respond to others with virtually no space or time limitations (Stroble, 1988). It is possible to set up an inexpensive network system within a classroom or school. This may satisfy short-term needs of students. However, long distance computer networks, information utilities, electronic bulletin boards, and mail services, although more expensive, have many more capabilities and provide more opportunities for communicating with a variety of audiences. As an illustration, Levin and his colleagues (1985) used a computer network to establish a pen pal program between youngsters in San Diego and Alaska. They later expanded their program to include the Computer Chronicles Newswire, a computer-supported school newspaper that allowed students from different locales to communicate about a variety of topics and issues ranging from life-style to school events. Improvements were noted in students' ability to tailor writing to their audience and produce compositions that were judged superior to those written exclusively for teachers to grade (Cohen and Riel, 1986). Results of their program, described in Chapter Four, are promising.

Conclusion

Specific instruction in writing processes needs to be combined with word processing instruction not only to capitalize on the knowledge of writers and to enhance their skill development, but also to capitalize on the strengths of the computer. As technology becomes more sophisticated, more options for computer writing will become available to students and instructors. Research in writing technology will likely be driven, in part, by current practice. That is, research will continue to lag behind technological advances in the field simply because it cannot keep pace with the phenomenal rate of technological change. Rather than attempt to justify every modification and feature in writing software, it may be more productive to identify the variables that appear to be effective for certain groups of learners or writers and then provide this information to software developers. For example, research on computers and writing instruction at the University of Maryland focuses on learning disabled youngsters (MacArthur, 1988). Information about the effects of computer-assisted composing on written language for this population should substantially influence the design of writing software intended to assist students with learning disabilities.

The foci on cognitive and metacognitive aspects of writing, instructional practices, and classroom conditions will have a significant impact on computer-based writing instruction. The microcomputer, primarily because of its interactive nature, has the potential not only to help us learn more about the processes that individuals use during writing, but also to learn about the instructional variables that influence the development of writing. We are just beginning to understand features of word processing that are not only appealing to writers and teachers, but also have the potential to improve writing instruction in our schools. The next three chapters will focus on computer-assisted composing research and instruction for elementary, secondary, and special needs writers.

CHAPTER 4

Computers and Writing at the Elementary Level

Writing, like other complex cognitive activities, requires the coordination and integration of a variety of mental processes. As children mature, it is assumed they will gradually acquire skills and abilities necessary for written expression. However, results of the recent National Assessment of Educational Progress (Applebee, Langer, and Mullis, 1986) suggest that, despite the writing instruction received in school, many students in elementary and secondary school lack skills required to communicate effectively in writing. Researchers and educators who study the development of writing in children are beginning to identify the cognitive characteristics of writers and explore instructional variables that affect writing development. As we learn more about the interaction of cognitive abilities, the development of written language, and the writing process, it becomes increasingly apparent that children will not become effective writers without instruction in writing processes.

Traditionally, elementary school children have been taught basic writing skills including handwriting, sentence patterns, grammar, mechanics, spelling, and the rudiments of composition. These basic skills, although important to the overall development of writing, often are taught in isolation, without regard for the context in which they are used. In contrast to traditional writing instruction, writing process instruction (Flower and Hayes, 1986; Graves, 1983; Bereiter and Scardamalia, 1987) emphasizes the integration and interaction of various cognitive processes that are the foundation for effective writing. Much of the research on writing, including computer-assisted composing, approaches the developing writer from a cognitive framework and an ecological perspective. This research supports the need to understand both the cognitive and metacognitive processes underlying writing ability and the interaction of the writer with the environment. These variables must be important considerations when designing curriculum and learning environments for beginning writers.

Writing instruction in the elementary grades is the focus of this chapter. First, to understand the development of writing processes and strategies in young children, writing research in the elementary grades is summarized. Research in computer-assisted composing for this age group then is reviewed. This research addresses primarily how computers mediate writing processes in children and how computer-based writing environments enhance the development and influence the interactions and attitudes of children. Learning and teaching strategies and curricular considerations also are discussed as they apply to computer-assisted composing in the elementary grades.

Writing Research

During the developmental years, between the ages of four and eleven, children acquire a host of cognitive strategies that enable them to solve problems across a variety of domains. General and specific problem-solving strategies are learned and applied to academic areas such as reading and writing. The goal of instruction at this level is acquisition, mastery, and automaticity of academic skills and strategies. As children mature, metacognitive or self-regulation strategies become more prominent. Students become more conscious of cognitive activity and learn to monitor and control strategy use. Although there is some evidence of early development of metacognitive strategies, appropriate and controlled application of such strategies is thought to occur later, sometime near the onset of adolescence (Flavell, 1985).

According to cognitive psychologists, during the elementary years, children acquire both general and domain-specific knowledge, actively engage in knowledge construction, and begin to acquire processes necessary for accessing knowledge. These processes are relatively undeveloped in young children, who frequently evidence considerable difficulty in gaining access to knowledge and generating content when writing. Children at this level also have relatively undeveloped memory search strategies. Ineffective memory search adversely affects ability to bring forth knowledge and information. Trial-and-error search strategies rather than systematic approaches to retrieving content from memory are characteristic of children at this age. Because their metacognitive abilities are just beginning to emerge during this period, elementary school children usually do not establish writing goals or engage in planning strategies typical of more experienced writers.

Marlene Scardamalia and Carl Bereiter are well known for their work on the development of writing strategies and processes of children in elementary school. Much of the following discussion relates directly to the work conducted by their team of researchers at the Ontario Institute for Studies in Education. These authors proposed a model of immature composing processes using a writing strategy termed the "knowledge telling strategy" (Scardamalia and Bereiter, 1986). This strategy, represented in Figure 4.1, reflects elementary children's basic approach to writing, whereby they simply tell all they know about a topic. Generally, if cued or prompted to write more, children will proceed using a process of association, which depends on "spreading activation, rather than a goal-directed, heuristic search process" (Scardamalia and Bereiter, 1986, p. 786). Encouraging children to continue writing after they have seemingly written everything they can appears to substantially increase production (Scardamalia, Bereiter, and Goelman, 1982) and, additionally, to increase the likelihood of information and knowledge recall from subordinate as well as from higher-level nodes in memory networks (McCutchen and Perfetti, 1982).

Developing schemata for writing is perhaps most fundamental to developing writing processes. Planning, composing, and revision activities are carried out in concordance with cognitive

Figure 4.1.
A model of text-generation according to the knowledge-telling strategy

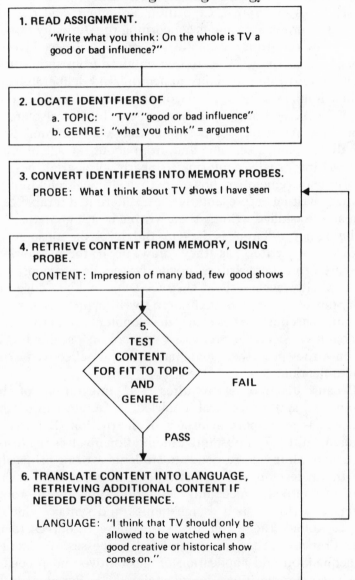

1. READ ASSIGNMENT.

"Write what you think: On the whole is TV a good or bad influence?"

2. LOCATE IDENTIFIERS OF

    a. TOPIC: "TV" "good or bad influence"
    b. GENRE: "what you think" = argument

3. CONVERT IDENTIFIERS INTO MEMORY PROBES.

PROBE: What I think about TV shows I have seen

4. RETRIEVE CONTENT FROM MEMORY, USING PROBE.

CONTENT: Impression of many bad, few good shows

5. TEST CONTENT FOR FIT TO TOPIC AND GENRE.

FAIL

PASS

6. TRANSLATE CONTENT INTO LANGUAGE, RETRIEVING ADDITIONAL CONTENT IF NEEDED FOR COHERENCE.

LANGUAGE: "I think that TV should only be allowed to be watched when a good creative or historical show comes on."

Source: M. Scardamalia and C. Bereiter, "Research on written composition." Reprinted with permission of Macmillan Publishing Company from *Handbook of Research on Teaching,* M. C. Wittrock, Editor. Copyright 1985 by American Educational Research Association.

schemata, to which writers must have access. Scardamalia and Bereiter (1986, p. 783) contend that "a major requirement for competence in writing is learning the essential form of various literary types—narrative, exposition, argument, and the like." Although there is agreement concerning the difficulty of young children in acquiring discourse schema knowledge, investigations of this attribute indicate that children from about the age of ten demonstrate the ability to acquire and deliberately draw on their implicit schema knowledge (Scardamalia and Bereiter, 1986). By the end of the primary grades, children also are able to produce narrative compositions that conform well to the narrative discourse schema; and, from about the age of ten on, their writing usually conforms to nearly all genre types. It is important to remember, however, that although children may produce writing representative of different literary genre, compared to skilled writers, their writing is still immature. One of the major differences lies in the level of consciousness displayed by writers as they draw upon their knowledge. Compared to expert writers, novice writers do not consciously and explicitly access their abstract schema knowledge. This ability must be nurtured as children's writing processes mature. The emphasis during these early developmental years should be on cognitive strategies to assist writers in "scaffolding" or building the processes and patterns for effective written communication.

Because composing requires the integration of both substantive and procedural knowledge, facilitation of these processes is an important aspect of instruction (Bereiter and Scardamalia, 1987). Substantive facilitation involves the teacher as a collaborator who responds to students' writing primarily to help them develop self-evaluative and meaning-level revision skills. In contrast, procedural facilitation supports the routine aspects of writing, such as mechanics and syntax, which, in essence, allows the writer to devote more resources to idea generation and other content-related processes. To facilitate the acquisition and application of substantive and procedural knowledge for writing, Scardamalia and Bereiter (1986) developed several innovative techniques, including a method, "simulation by intervention," to investigate the effects of certain types of facilitation on the writing processes of students. In a series of procedural facilitation studies, children were asked to identify and diagnose problems based on a fixed set of diagnoses and then, either during or after writing, select remedies for the problems. Intervention studies such as these that provide procedural level supports for solving composition problems have led to more appropriate and higher-level revisions resulting in better quality compositions by elementary school children (Cohen and Scardamalia, 1983; Scardamalia and Bereiter, 1983, 1986).

Computer writing tools can provide a variety of supports to assist in the construction of both substantive and procedural knowledge for writing. These tools, therefore, have important implications for improving writing instruction. The next section examines computer-assisted composing research conducted with elementary children during the past several years.

Computer-Assisted Composing Research

The effects of word processing and other computer tools on writing is a relatively new field of inquiry. Only within the last fifteen years has practical, feasible, cost-efficient computer hardware and software for classroom use been available to schools. Microcomputers and software tools that are efficient, user-friendly, and powerful are becoming increasingly obtainable. Many of these tools are being developed to facilitate writing for elementary youngsters. Like other new educational materials, these tools must be tested to validate their effectiveness and determine their usefulness for improving children's composing skills. Teachers must be assured that these writing tools will enhance rather than disrupt instruction and that students indeed will benefit from computer-assisted composing.

In the early 1980s, researchers began to examine various aspects of computer-assisted composing. They were interested not only in the effects of word processing on the development of writing processes and the written production of students, but also in the attitudes of students and teachers toward this mode of instruction and the effects of computer-assisted composing on the interactional patterns of students and teachers. Another major concern among researchers was the identification of variables that affect the cognitive and metacognitive processes associated with written composition. Discussed in this section will be several research foci, including acquisition of keyboarding skills; effects of word processing and other writing tools on writing performance; effects on the draft process with particular concern for surface level and content level revisions; effects on attitudes, learning patterns, and collaborative skills of students; and, finally, effects of voice synthesis on the acquisition of reading and writing skills of children.

Keyboard Skills

To offset concerns that learning to type or use keyboard commands for word processing may interfere with the acquisition of composing skills, a few computer-assisted composing studies have looked at the acquisition of keyboard skills. These studies have found that even young children can master the fundamentals of word processing with little special training (Beal and Griffin, 1987; Daiute, 1985b; Kurth and Kurth, 1987). Daiute's (1985b) studies indicated that children as young as six years remember commands, learn positions of keys on the keyboard, and type sentences, whereas children over eight years of age can memorize the keys and learn to "touch type." In a study with kindergarten and first-grade children, Kurth and Kurth (1987) found that children easily adapted to the keyboard and had little difficulty acquiring the simple commands and patterns of word processing. Beal and Griffin (1987) taught twenty-five third- and fourth-grade students to use the MacWrite text editor in four 20 to 30 minute sessions and compared the use of the mouse with keyboard. All of the fourth graders and 80 percent of the third graders learned the basic keyboard commands by the end of the first session. It is interesting that the children in this study found the mouse more difficult to use than the keyboard commands. In another study, fourth graders were provided with instruction in both keyboarding and word processing or were provided with word processing instruction only (Gerlach, 1987). The author found no discernible differences between the groups in the length of their compositions, the total number and type of revisions made, or their attitudes toward using the word processor for writing. However, results showed the keyboard tutorial group to be superior to the word processing only group in typing speed and accuracy after using computers under supervision for a period of four months.

Learning to use a word processor may not be as physically demanding as was assumed. It seems that, for most children, learning to use a keyboard is a relatively facile and enjoyable activity. Students in the third or fourth grade should be able to learn basic word processing commands even for fairly sophisticated programs. As students progress in school, they can then learn additional features as needed. Although elementary school children have little difficulty adapting to computer keyboards and seem to profit from direct instruction in keyboard skills as they learn to compose on a computer, there are some caveats to consider when selecting word processing programs for them. Daiute (1985b) recommended programs with on-screen editing, programmed function keys, single keystroke commands, and labeled command keys to facilitate teaching and learning keyboard skills. Tutorials are available either separately or as a component of word processing programs to provide keyboard instruction for individuals of all ages. The Appendix lists several keyboard tutorial programs.

Writing Performance

The most salient concern of researchers studying computer-assisted composing has been the effects of word processing on the quality of students' writing. Studies generally confirm that children write more when using a computer than with pencil and paper. Similar positive effects in the quality of compositions, however, have not always been found. Although the majority of studies indicate improvement in quality (Roblyer, Castine, and King, 1988), some have found no discernible qualitative differences when comparing computer-assisted composing with pencil and paper composing (e.g., Daiute, 1985b, Miller, 1985; Woolley, 1986). These equivocal results have raised questions about the benefits of using computers for writing instruction. It therefore is necessary as well as useful to review the accumulating evidence regarding the effectiveness of computer-assisted composing to identify techniques that positively affect children's writing performance.

Rather than simply testing the effects of word processing on writing behavior, several researchers have chosen to study word processing as a vehicle for writing in combination with writing process instruction. In an intervention study involving 204 fourth and fifth graders, Moore (1987) found that a developmental writing program incorporating writing process instruction significantly improved the quality of compositions by students who used word processors as compared with students who used pencil and paper. Burnett (1986) also noted an improvement in quality as well as fluency of writing when word processing was used in conjunction with a writing process approach to instruction. There was some indication from the results of this study that the level and type of interaction between students and teachers during writing conferences may be different when word processing is used, and this difference may have contributed to overall improvements in writing. Through observation of first-grade children engaged in computer-assisted composing, Phenix and Hannan (1984) found that children wrote longer pieces, continued to write on pieces produced on previous days, had more conferences with their teachers about writing, included more detail in their writing, revised more, and seemed to be more involved in the writing process. Furthermore, students' transcribing skills, spacing, printing, and spelling improved. These results are encouraging as they support the use of word processing within the context of writing process instruction.

Conferences, which are a component of writing process instruction, and collaboration, which often is a by-product of this instructional approach, seems to be positively associated with writing quality (Daiute, 1985b; Dickinson, 1986; Riel, 1983). Studies conducted with primary school children support the use of this model for teaching beginning writing skills. For example, after integrating a computer into a first- and second-grade writing program, Dickinson (1986) reported that the teacher emphasized idea sharing and evaluating and used writing process instruction across the curriculum. Over the course of one semester, the researcher analyzed the emergence of cooperation and collaboration in the classroom, considered the role of the computer in fostering this development, and analyzed the effects of collaboration on interaction during writing time. Findings from this ethnographic study indicated that collaborative work at the computer appeared to create a new social organization that affected interaction patterns, increased the amount of talk about text meaning and what was being written, and led to error detection in peers' writing. Another study found that collaborative writing and word processing improved first-grade students' ability to write, alter a document, and read the document upon completion (Heap, 1986).

Daiute (1985b), in a series of word processing studies, found that children thought writing on a computer is easier and more fun than using pencil and paper primarily because it eliminates recopying compositions. Additionally, children generally wrote more and stayed with the writing task for longer periods of time. Positive attitudes toward computer-assisted composing also were reported by Cheever (1987), Boone (1986), and Fernandez (1988). The elementary children in these studies expressed a preference for using the computer rather than pencil and paper for writing. They also reported writing more on their own and showed positive attitudes toward revising.

Studies on revision patterns of children using a word processor provide some intriguing insights into the writing processes of children. Some studies reported minimal effects for editing and revision, particularly with regard to meaning or content level revision (Beal and Griffin, 1987; Schanck, 1986). By and large, however, researchers reported positive effects on children's revision processes and patterns in terms of both mechanics and the content of their writing (Boone, 1986; Cheever, 1987; Kaplan, 1986; Moore, 1987). Although spelling checkers and text editors hold great promise for reducing the demands placed on writers during editing and revision, there seems to be a consensus to avoid their use with children in the primary grades. Indeed, it may be best to virtually ignore errors in mechanics and spelling in kindergarten and early first grade or until children have made the transition from speech to writing and internalized the idea of writing. Then, computer prompting programs such as QUILL (Rubin and Bruce, 1984) or CATCH (Daiute, 1985b) can be introduced. These programs were designed especially for young learners and have been used successfully with elementary school children to increase both quantity and quality of their revisions.

Another innovative and promising approach to computer-assisted composing uses voice synthesis in combination with word processing. By connecting a speech synthesizer to the computer, children can opt to hear what they write as they compose or read through a completed composition. Several researchers have studied this approach to developing early writing skills. Word processors with voice synthesizers fostered collaborative writing for kindergarten and first-grade children in one study by Kurth and Kurth (1987) and led to increased levels of editing for second graders in another by Borgh and Dickson (1986). Rosegrant (1986) also studied the use of a talking word processor with primary level children over a 6 month period and discovered that children spent more time writing, made more revisions, and produced longer and higher quality texts.

The results of a study with prekindergarten and kindergarten children (Lehrer et al., 1987) suggested that voice-aided word processing acted as a scaffold for young children's composition by promoting the acquisition of several components of preschool literacy including symbol-sound and sound-symbol associations. There also was evidence this method made children more aware of the communicative purposes and processes of writing. Additionally, they thought more about their topic before writing, developed text that corresponded to their phonetic understandings of words, and sequenced their ideas to conform to conversational conventions. The authors concluded that computer-assisted composing may actually facilitate the transition from speech to writing by reducing the physical constraints associated with learning to write. Word processing, either alone or in combination with other computer-assisted composing tools—and, most notably, in combination with writing process instruction—seems to enhance writing for elementary school children. The remainder of this chapter highlights several learning and teaching strategies for computer-assisted composing.

Learning Strategies

By building on what children already know, teachers can assist children in becoming competent writers and help them develop and refine composition skills. Computer-assisted composing, particularly when paired with writing process instruction, can increase elementary children's knowledge and use of cognitive and metacognitive strategies.

Scardamalia's and Bereiter's (1986) "knowledge telling strategy" captures the immature writer's approach to composing (see Figure 4.1). This model of text generation consists of six basic steps:

1. Read the assignment.

2. Locate the identifiers of the topic and genre.

3. Convert the identifiers into memory probes.

4. Use the probes to retrieve content from memory.

5. Test the content for its fit to the topic and genre.

6. Translate the content into language, retrieving additional content if it is needed for coherence.

The knowledge telling strategy is a basic, linear, and unidimensional approach to composition. Although this strategy may be used by expert writers, it represents a low-level choice among the range of writing strategies. As an immature approach to writing, it is characterized by limited planning and goal setting, use of free association, and undeveloped revision processes. Children typically revise minimally and usually at the surface level, with revisions consisting primarily of changes in mechanics and spelling rather than in content. However immature these writing patterns are, they serve as the basis for developing cognitive and metacognitive processes and, therefore, must be fostered and extended during writing instruction. Regardless of the level of the learner, instruction should be structured around the process model of writing and should capitalize on the developing composition skills of children. The knowledge telling strategy can be expanded by introducing criteria to test content or by requiring writers to engage in some type of planning activity prior to writing (Scardamalia and Bereiter, 1986).

Computers can be a valuable tool in developing planning processes in children. Young writers frequently engage in simple, concrete activities or strategies to prepare for writing (Graves, 1983). They may draw a picture of their story, act it out, rehearse it, or simply tell part of the story before beginning to write. Software such as Logowriter (Wilburg, 1988) or Story Maker (Rubin and Bruce, 1984), which incorporate these kinds of strategies, can be used to engage children in early planning activities. Logowriter permits the integration of text and graphics, whereas Story Maker allows students to construct stories by selecting already written story parts. At this level, the stage is set for developing the concept of planning throughout the writing process. We know that most beginning writers use the knowledge telling strategy as their primary production strategy. However, this strategy does not have a planning component and does not provide for explicit goal formulation. Therefore, it is important that instruction incorporate procedures to develop goal-oriented writing, while encouraging production abilities.

Just as children develop cognitive processes, they also acquire knowledge and construct schemata. Because children usually are unable to consciously acquire information and schemata and often are unaware of the knowledge they have, their compositions frequently contain only a portion of what they know. The advantage of the knowledge telling strategy is that, even when children indicate that they have written all they know about a topic, prompting them to write more increases their production and fluency, which, in turn, gives children personal satisfaction (Calkins, 1986). Computer prompting programs, such as QUILL and CATCH, encourage children to "tell more" or "give details" and provide necessary incentives to children as they elaborate on ideas and expand their writing. Through these kinds of activities, they become actively engaged in knowledge telling. Promoting this tendency of children to express what they know fosters other, more formal types of writing as writing processes mature.

Applebee (1986) advocated scaffolding to enhance composition skills in children. As defined in Chapter Three, scaffolds are supports that allow children to complete tasks by first understanding the problem and then selecting and executing specific strategies to solve it. Both substantive and procedural scaffolds must be provided to assist children in the internalization of routines and procedures as they mature and progress in their writing. Computer tools can enhance the development of substantive and procedural knowledge in children. Narrative writing is a good example of genre-based writing that can be mediated by software scaffolding strategies. By school entry, most children have the rudiments of story grammar in place (Mandler and Johnson, 1977; Stein and Glenn, 1979), and, by the end of the primary grades, they are producing well-formed narrative compositions (Scardamalia and Bereiter, 1986). A plethora of software is available for developing narrative writing skills. Using this software with young children who already are adept at creating stories may help refine their narrative writing skills and prepare them for the transition to other, less familiar genre. Just as voice synthesis coupled with word processing provides a kind of scaffold for beginning reading and writing skills in young children (Lehrer et al., 1987), genre-based courseware may provide the necessary scaffolds to enable children to bridge expressive and other types of writing such as essays and reports. Because children from about the age of ten on generally conform to all genre types (Scardamalia and Bereiter, 1986), other genre-based software should be introduced by the third or fourth grade.

The pragmatics of language is associated with the purpose of oral or written communication. This level of language is relatively undeveloped in elementary school children. Pragmatics refers to establishing clear writing goals, having a good sense of audience, and effectively evaluating one's own writing for cohesion, clarity, and adherence to purpose. Closely related to metacognition, the pragmatics of language, by its nature, is representative of higher-order thinking. Young children generally are not concerned about the purpose for their writing and show little control over it. Self-monitoring and self-control strategies are more characteristic of older, experienced writers who are able to detect surface level errors as well as content level inconsistencies in their writing. Because metacognitive strategies are developing during the elementary years, this level should be viewed as the transition period for the acquisition of higher-level processes. Teachers need to become familiar with cognitive and metacognitive processes and learning strategies that influence children's writing to plan appropriate instruction. It is important for teachers to be able to select teaching strategies that nurture and augment children's knowledge and use of writing strategies.

Teaching Strategies

A variety of effective teaching strategies facilitate planning, composing, and revision processes for elementary school children. Activities for planning compositions are analogous, in many respects, to prereading activities. For example, prereading activities assist children in recalling knowledge about a topic, setting a purpose for reading, and making connections between what they know and what they are reading. The rationale for prewriting or planning activities is similar. Children are given techniques and strategies to stimulate and intensify their knowledge awareness, goal development, and idea formation. Teachers can foster these aspects of composition planning by providing class discussion, small group and individual conferences, and computer courseware specifically designed to help children prepare for writing.

Computer-assisted composing software can be used by children individually or in small groups for brainstorming topics and ideas, free writing, generating ideas, and making word lists. One effective prewriting technique that could be adapted easily to computer composing has been investigated by Scardamalia and Bereiter (1986). They found that memory search was enhanced when students selected a topic and then generated isolated words that might be used during writing. Another effective search strategy that appears to aid goal development is writing toward a prescribed ending sentence (McCutchen and Perfetti, 1982). This technique seems to encourage children to develop an overall plan complete with supporting details that make sense in light of the story's concluding sentence.

Perhaps the most useful prewriting activity is prompting, a technique to guide children in text development. Computer prompting programs include electronic advance organizers, checklists, or sets of questions used to direct children in their writing. Planner, one of the components of the integrated computer program, QUILL, consists of activities designed to encourage children to take notes, write down ideas, and structure thoughts and ideas in preparation for writing (Rubin and Bruce, 1984). Daiute's (1985b) CATCH is another good example of a prompting program to aid students' planning and revision both during and after composing. This program offers comments, questions, and other analytic techniques for both surface and content level revision.

During the elementary years, teachers should introduce these programs gradually after children have had an opportunity to learn and practice various planning activities. Software designed to facilitate prewriting or planning activities is further described in the Appendix. Although some programs are suitable for young writers, most are more appropriate for intermediate level and older children who have already developed expressive writing skills.

Early composing experiences should allow children to write on a topic that excites and enthuses them. Graves (1983) found that if primary children have a strong desire to write about a topic, the length of their compositions increases; and Scardamalia and Bereiter (1982) found that simply urging children to write more actually doubles their production. Providing the opportunity for children to write more not only increases their fluency, but also gives them confidence. As children become comfortable expressing themselves in writing, they will begin to write longer pieces and return to their compositions at a later time to continue or revise their writing. When students reach this level of composing, they can be introduced to more formalized styles and different literary genre.

Several teaching strategies for encouraging expressive writing include journal writing, stories, personal experience narratives, and various communication activities that encourage children to write messages and respond to one another's writing. Classroom Chat (Collins, 1983), which is a computerized version of a personal problem-solving newspaper column, encourages children to write personal problem descriptions and respond to their classmates' problems and concerns by writing solutions. Classroom and long distance microcomputer networks also can dramatically influence the writing habits of children. As mentioned in Chapter Three, Levin and his colleagues (1985) have been experimenting for several years with a computer news network called the Computer Chronicle Newswire. This network allows students to communicate with other students in different schools both within their community and out-of-state. This program and other computerized writing programs emphasizing communication and audience participation are described more fully in the next section on the computer writing environment.

The teacher as collaborator must provide stimulating writing experiences for children, which enhance growth and development of cognitive and metacognitive processes integral to the composing process. As mentioned earlier, both substantive and procedural facilitation can stimulate the writing processes of children. Substantive facilitation techniques focus on textual content and include probes and cues as well as direct responses to what the child says or writes. One of the mainstays of writing process instruction is the teacher's use of nonspecific cues, prompts, and questions throughout the process. Additionally, children should be provided both general and specific feedback about their writing.

In contrast to substantive facilitation, which primarily addresses the content of a composition, procedural facilitation focuses on the mechanics and style of writing. Word processors offer a certain kind of procedural facilitation by freeing the writer to concentrate on substance by simplifying the mechanical aspects of writing (Daiute, 1985b). Procedural supports such as spelling checkers and text analyzers may inhibit or interfere with the performance of children who are just learning to express themselves in writing. That is the main reason why these computer tools should be introduced only when children are comfortable with the writing process and have developed some written expression skills.

Collaboration with both teachers and peers is highly recommended during all phases of the writing process. For young children, the most important time for collaboration is before they actually begin writing. This helps stimulate their imaginations and aids in idea formulation. Having children share their writing with other students is another important part of the writing process, particularly if teachers identify clarification and refinement of ideas as the purpose behind this part of the process (Graves, 1983; Calkins, 1986). Computer-assisted composing is conducive to collaboration in writing as it enables children to cooperatively create, print, and distribute text for audience reaction. As noted earlier, mechanical, grammatical, and spelling errors, for the most part, should be overlooked in young children's writing. It is necessary, however, to teach the draft process to children so they become accustomed to returning to their compositions to modify and clarify their expression of ideas as well as correct mechanical and other types of surface errors. Again, as children begin to make progress in their composing, specific revision strategies should be taught and computer revision and editing software introduced.

Various writing strategies can be adapted easily to computer-assisted composing and can provide executive support to students as they make the transition to metacognitive activities. One such strategy requires students to stop after each sentence to evaluate it and decide if revision is needed. If revision seems necessary, they are given the opportunity to select and execute a previously learned revision strategy. Another procedure involves reading the whole text, placing markers where problems are detected, and then diagnosing and selecting remedies. Both procedures provide students with an evaluation routine and a preestablished set of diagnoses from which to choose. These self-monitoring activities have been effective in eliciting higher level evaluations of students' own writing and also higher level revisions (Scardamalia and Bereiter, 1983, 1985). Revision strategies should be taught before presenting computer text editors and analyzers to help students conceptualize and internalize the processes associated with textual revision. Establishing a positive, accommodating climate for writing is important to the development of skills. The next section addresses various environmental considerations for elementary school writers.

Computer Writing Environment

Much of the research in computer-assisted composing has considered to some degree the environmental context for writing. In addition to understanding the effects of word processing and other computer tools on writing processes and products, researchers also are concerned with identifying the contextual variables that affect students' performance and attitude. Results of a study to assess the environment for computer writing in a fourth-grade classroom (Reid, 1986) suggested that the computer has an impact on the environment through its interactions with the writer, task, and context and acts as a catalyst within the writing environment that transforms writing from a private to a public activity.

Mehan, Miller-Souviney, and Riel (1984) concluded from their study that the new social organization made possible by the computer was responsible for the positive effects on children's reading and writing processes. Moreover, they claimed that the integration of the computer into the language arts curriculum established a functional learning environment in which the purpose of reading and writing as communicative activities became clear. By studying the effects of a functional writing environment on the composing processes of children, these authors specified several variables that appear to affect students' performance and attitudes toward writing. This writing environment, alluded to earlier in this chapter, is structured around the Computer Chronicles Newswire, a computer network that connects classroom computer stations from Alaska, California, Hawaii, and Mexico. In this environment, students at each site write articles, which are stored on floppy disks and sent to participating schools. Newspapers using articles from a variety of sites including the home site then are published and shared across the network. Message exchange among students is an integral part of the system. As students control the writing process, they develop a sense of audience by sharing ideas and information with local and distant persons. Because they write for an audience, children are motivated to make both surface and content level revisions to clarify their ideas. The authors reasoned that as students enlarge their communicative sphere, their conceptualization of the writing process changes. Within this functional writing context, students seemed to prefer the word processor to pencil and paper for writing, became accustomed to collaborative writing, and also became skilled text editors.

Publication of children's writing, as part of writing process instruction, contributes strongly to the writers' development (Graves, 1983). The print capabilities of a computer writing environment simplify manuscript revision during the composing process and make possible professional looking publications that can be shared by other children, teachers, and parents. Desktop publishing motivates students to perfect their texts before submitting them for "publication." Students begin to take their editorial responsibilities seriously if publication is part of the writing environment. Publisher, another subprogram of QUILL (Rubin and Bruce, 1984), is designed to publish not only class newspapers but also books. The program has formats for messages, memos, and personal letters. Computer programs such as this can do much to stimulate and motivate students to write.

Approximately 70 percent of the elementary school day is devoted to language arts instruction in the form of listening, speaking, reading, and writing activities (Madian, 1986). With this in mind, it is reasonable to assume that a computer-based writing environment has the potential to revolutionize the entire language arts curriculum and change the face of language arts instruction. Researchers are beginning to investigate the impact of the computer writing environment not only as it affects the performance and attitudes of students, but also as it alters the nature of instruction. As an illustration of this trend, Henney (1988) introduced the Story Tree computer program into the language arts curriculum of fifth and sixth graders. In this writing program, students wrote stories for second and third grade students. As the project progressed, two of the three classroom teachers involved in the study gave up their regular skills-based language arts instructional time for the story writing program. The teachers attributed this change to a realization that students were getting practice in all the language arts skills in an integrated environment where writing was stimulating and challenging. This study represents the next generation of research on computer-assisted composing in its focus on ways in which the computer writing environment can accommodate competency-based language arts instruction and meet established curricular objectives, yet not sacrifice the stimulation and creativity of the writing process.

Conclusion

Although computer-assisted composing rapidly is becoming a reality in many classrooms, research is just beginning to validate the effectiveness of word processing and adjunct computer writing tools. It is clear from the research, however, that word processing is a natural partner for writing process instruction. Research in writing and computer-assisted composing provides insight into the many ways in which the computer can be used to facilitate writing processes for elementary children by promoting their use of cognitive and metacognitive strategies. Research also provides insight into instructional practices that are beneficial for writers of different ages and provides direction for the creation of effective computer writing environments. The foundation for writing is established during the elementary years. The needs of students change at the secondary level, as they begin to refine their composing processes and develop nature writing strategies. Computer-assisted composing at the secondary level is the subject of the next chapter.

CHAPTER 5

Computers and Writing at the Secondary Level

As children progress through school, they make numerous developmental and psychological adaptations to the environmental and curricular changes that typify transitions across grade levels. Perhaps the most notable transition with which children must cope in school is associated with the academic curriculum, which undergoes a gradual shift from instruction in basic skills to content area instruction. At the secondary school level, the expectations for students are vastly different from those at the elementary school level. By junior high school, students are expected to have acquired basic skills in the three R's and be prepared to apply those skills successfully across the curriculum. As a result of this curricular change, new demands are placed on students. In secondary school, for instance, the emphasis in reading is no longer on learning to read, but rather on reading to learn. A similar shift in expectations occurs for writing. Although secondary school teachers may devote some time in language arts classes to teaching elements of writing such as sentence structure and grammar, they clearly expect students, particularly at the senior high level, to be fluent, capable writers who can articulate their ideas in an organized, cohesive manner. Students must be able to demonstrate an ability to communicate effectively through writing. Despite these expectations, students in today's schools generally are poor writers and can produce only the simplest compositions.

According to a recent National Assessment of Educational Progress report on writing achievement, "fewer than one-fourth of the students in grade 11 performed adequately on writing tasks involving skills required for success in academic studies, business, or the professions" (Applebee, Langer, and Mullis, 1986).

There are several plausible explanations for students' poor writing performance. First, traditional writing instruction stresses spelling, mechanics, neatness, and handwriting. Teachers typically spend an inordinate amount of time on these aspects of writing and often teach these skills in isolation, apart from composition. Additionally, little time is given to instruction in writing processes in the traditional writing curriculum. Consequently, students usually do not plan what they are going to write; generally have limited resources for formulating, generating, and organizing their ideas; and rarely revise their compositions. Finally, although students are expected to be effective communicators in writing, in most classes their only audience is the teacher, who "corrects" the errors and then requires students to recopy their teacher-corrected compositions. Students learn little from this exercise other than that writing is tedious, with little relevance to activities outside of school. The poor performance of secondary school students surely is an indication that traditional writing instruction does not meet the needs of the majority of students in our schools.

Applebee (1981) contended that writers at the secondary level do not learn to see writing as a recursive process, do not believe that writing is useful, do not engage in challenging and thoughtful writing in school, and spend little time composing in school. To effect change in the schools, teachers must become aware of the characteristics of adolescent writers, the inadequacies of the traditional writing curriculum, and the features of writing process instruction that are most beneficial for writing instruction in secondary schools. It is essential that teachers become familiar with computer-assisted composing as a method for involving students in the writing process. Perhaps even more than at the elementary level, writing instruction at the secondary level is shifting to computer-assisted instruction that not only aids students in the development of writing processes, but also encourages interaction and communication among learners.

This chapter reviews research in both writing and computer-assisted composing. Attributes that make writing instruction more effective for this level of learner and various strategies for learning and teaching composition are identified. Finally, several suggestions for establishing a computer writing environment in secondary schools are presented.

Writing Research

In Chapter Four, writing characteristics of elementary school children were discussed, and particular attention was given to the development and interaction of cognitive strategies during the act of writing. It was noted that children characteristically rely on a linear approach to writing. That is, they typically use trial-and-error strategies for memory search and an immature "knowledge telling" or associative strategy for composing. Awareness of processes and access to knowledge are limited for young writers, who are concerned primarily with writing everything they think they know about a topic. In elementary school, general and specific strategies are acquired as a foundation is laid for the development of higher-level cognitive strategies and metacognitive or self-regulation strategies. Metacognitive processes such as planning, self-monitoring, and meaning-level revision begin to surface by the fourth and fifth grade. By the end of elementary school, even though children have not mastered the mechanics and conventions of writing, they usually have developed efficient executive controls for switching attention between mechanical and substantive concerns (Scardamalia and Bereiter, 1986). As writers mature, their cognitive and metacognitive processes become refined, and cognitive overload due to surface level concerns no longer seems to be a problem.

The research conducted by Carl Bereiter and Marlene Scardamalia (1987) at the Ontario Institute for Studies in Education provides much of what is known about the development of writing processes in early adolescence. Their findings across multiple studies suggest that between grades six and eight children begin to show evidence of working at a more abstract level during text production and also begin to demonstrate ability to plan at the level of conceptualization.

There is evidence that instruction in planning benefits older learners by assisting in idea formation and organization, whereas planning instruction for younger learners usually leads to simple content generation or knowledge telling (Haas, 1988). Perhaps the main advantage that older learners have over younger learners is their ability to activate metacognitive processes that come into play during composing. By adolescence, students are becoming more conscious of the cognitive activities needed to complete tasks. Sometime between grades four and ten, students can be expected to begin making the transition from simple content generation as a planning strategy to a form of planning that is more conceptual in nature. Taking notes and outlining are examples of such conceptual planning activities. Despite their "cognitive readiness," the majority of writers in secondary school appear to plan infrequently, however. National Assessment of Educational Progress results showed less than 25 percent of students in grade 11 actually using notes as a planning strategy to formulate persuasive letters (Applebee et al., 1986). For the students who do take notes, transformations from notes to text have been observed. One study found that by age fourteen, students did not incorporate notes into text without some major change occurring in the form of elaboration, reordering, combination, or addition (Burtis et al., 1983). It seems that by secondary school, students are more flexible in their thinking, are better equipped to juggle thoughts and ideas, and are able to operate at a more abstract level when tapping their memory and when forming and organizing ideas.

In contrast to trial and error strategies used by young writers to retrieve information from their memory, more sophisticated memory search strategies characteristically are used by older writers. There is evidence that both metamemorial search and heuristic search strategies begin to appear in students from about the age of twelve (Scardamalia and Bereiter, 1986). Metamemorial search is concerned with determining the availability of information in memory. Scardamalia and Bereiter (1986) found that, when given a general topic for writing, twelve-year-olds were able to use rudimentary metamemorial search strategies to select a specific topic for their composition. Heuristic search, on the other hand, is aimed at reducing the extent of search by taking advantage of and extending partial knowledge. Heuristic search strategies typically are associated with writers' ability to conform to specific genres and the ability to establish and write toward goals. These types of memory search patterns, although more characteristic of older writers, can be found to some extent among younger writers, who, when provided with writing supports such as topic sentences and memory cues, frequently exhibit some level of metamemorial or heuristic search activity.

Similar to the concerns of writing researchers who work with younger children, research concerns regarding secondary level students also focus on cognitive and metacognitive processes employed during the composing process. It is encouraging that many writing researchers at this level have begun to study the effects of computer-assisted composing on these writing processes. The influences of different types of computer writing environment on students as they become involved in the composing process are being investigated as well.

Computer-Assisted Composing Research

Interest in developing software to facilitate composition instruction at the elementary, secondary, and college levels has been the driving force behind much of the research in computer-assisted composing (Wresch, 1984a). Research and development projects proliferated during the past decade as evidenced by the number of computer programs now available to facilitate writing by students. The Appendix contains many examples of computer-assisted composing software currently on the market. Both word processing programs and integrated composing packages were developed and field tested to identify their most effective properties and to eliminate "bugs." These early studies are valuable in that they provide the basis for current research in this area. Efforts continue to be directed toward understanding how software augments composition instruction. A knowledge base is accumulating on the cognitive characteristics and behavioral patterns of students as they compose on the computer. Research conducted with secondary level writers, like that with younger students, addresses both the academic and affective responses of students to computer tools. Of primary interest is the effect of computer-assisted composing on the development of students' writing processes. Another interest is how students interact with computers, teachers, and peers within a computer writing environment.

Writing process instruction has been the focus of several computer-assisted composing studies with secondary students. The value of pairing writing process instruction with word processing is becoming increasingly apparent to advocates of computer-based instruction. In a study of 176 eighth graders, Sweeney (1986) found that students produced significantly superior expository essays when provided with a combination of the composition process method and word processing. Results of another study involving high-average ninth-grade students also supported the combination of word processing and writing process instruction (Kurth, 1987). In this study, two groups of students were taught prewriting, draft writing, revising, and editing skills and then wrote four compositions. Students were given the opportunity to write as many drafts as they wanted, and also were assigned to editing groups who reviewed the compositions and assisted the writer with revisions. The group who used word processing produced substantially longer compositions. It must be remembered, however, that longer essays do not necessarily imply higher-quality writing.

Some researchers have investigated the primary effects of word processing on writing performance of secondary students without attempting to manipulate the method of instruction. Results, although somewhat equivocal, seem to favor word processing as a vehicle for writing. Studies with remedial writers at the secondary level generally support the use of word processing over pen and paper (Cirello, 1987; Dalton and Hannafin, 1987; Dalton and Watson, 1986; Pivarnik, 1986). Investigations of average and above average learners, however, have produced unclear results regarding the superiority of word processing over traditional pen and pencil writing (Bigley, 1987; Bryson, 1986; Dalton and Watson, 1986; Kurth, 1987; Lytle,

1988). There is speculation that positive effects may not always be detected due to writers' lack of experience with keyboarding and word processing. Just as poor handwriting inhibits written expression, poor keyboard skills also may interfere with one's ability to get thoughts down on paper. Monahan (1986) conducted an interesting study comparing computer science high school students with students trained in word processing only and found no significant differences between the groups except that the computer science students used more word processing features than the other group. It may be that prior computer experience accelerates acquisition of keyboard and word processing skills.

Results of several studies of the revision processes of secondary students who use word processing suggest that word processing generally promotes surface level revision, but does little to enhance content or meaning level revision (e.g., Lytle, 1988). Interestingly, though, findings from other studies of revision patterns suggest that students are capable of making content level revisions and frequently do (Pearson and Wilkinson, 1986; Womble, 1984). Daiute (1986), in her study of seventh- and ninth-grade students, detected different revision patterns for computer composing than for pen and paper when students were provided with revision prompts. Students who did not have the advantage of prompts tended to rely on a knowledge telling strategy. Rather than concentrate on global text revisions, they simply added more words to the end of their texts and corrected more word and sentence level errors. In contrast, students who used a revision prompting program attached to the word processing program generally made more revisions at both levels. These students also balanced their revisions within and at the end of the composition. The author concluded that word processing enabled students to skim the text for errors and inconsistencies and then improve it by adding words to the end, while revision prompting enabled students to interact with the text, making deeper level as well as surface level revision easier. This interactive component of revision may be necessary for students who are unfamiliar with revision and have little experience monitoring and modifying their writing. Lansing (1984) pointed out that students who have developed a reviser "style" in their writing may adapt more readily to computer-assisted composing than students who focus only on planning processes or those who rely on knowledge telling. She also indicated that, although students may enjoy working on a computer, they may not necessarily change their attitude toward writing. Although we are learning more about this aspect of computer-assisted composing, much of the research suggests that students' attitudes toward both computers and writing improve as a result of this approach to writing instruction.

Attitudinal research provides insight into the affective responses of students toward the computer as a writing tool and toward writing as a process. The eighth graders in an informal study by Stromberg and Kurth (1983) were positive about their word processing experiences and developed cooperative sharing attitudes that seemed to be enhanced by the writing laboratory environment. Other studies with secondary level students have noted an increase in motivation; greater peer involvement; and more positive attitudes toward instruction, writing ability, and revision (Bigley, 1987; Kurth, 1987; Profetto, 1987). Although the research in computer-assisted composing, particularly at the secondary level, has been limited, it nonetheless is evident that computer-assisted composing is a promising alternative to traditional modes of writing instruction. Especially when combined with writing process instruction, word processing can be an effective tool for composing for junior and senior high students. The following elements of a writing process milieu were identified by seniors as essential in an ethnographic study by Curtiss (1984): a meaningful writing topic, time to think and write, a place to think and write without distraction, valued feedback within the context of dialogue regarding one's writing, and word processing as a writing context. In addition to consideration for these instructional variables, teachers also must be attuned to instructional and learning strategies used by older students. These learning and teaching strategies must be systematically validated to maximize the benefits of computer-assisted composing to secondary students. The following section addresses the importance of learning and teaching strategies for writing.

Learning and Teaching Strategies

It was mentioned earlier that, beginning in junior high school, students are expected to apply skills and strategies that presumably were acquired during their elementary years. We also know how unrealistic it is to assume that all students in secondary school possess the necessary writing skills to produce coherent, cohesive compositions. Based on what is known about composition processes and the performance of students in secondary school, there is little doubt that writing process instruction is necessary to inculcate strategies and processes as students become competent, proficient writers. From this information, we can conclude that writing process instruction is as important at the secondary level as at the elementary level.

Perhaps the primary difference between the learning characteristics of students at the elementary level and those of students at the secondary level is their "readiness" for higher-level cognitive and metacognitive processing. Cognitive readiness is one of the intellectual attributes of older learners. Other attributes include an expanding knowledge base; a larger memory capacity; the availability of more sophisticated memory search strategies; greater access to a variety of cognitive strategies; and the ability to direct, regulate, and control cognitive functions. To make use of cognitive abilities, an individual must be able to operate at both conscious and subconscious levels as the task demands. Awareness of cognitive and metacognitive functions is one of the distinguishing features of mature individuals. Many high school students are unaware of their knowledge and learning strategies and, consequently, often do not apply what they know. Providing students with techniques to heighten awareness and to activate the knowledge, skills, and strategies already in place should improve their approach to writing tasks. In other words, teaching students to recognize, manage, and monitor cognitive activity is essential if they are to become efficient in the self-monitoring and self-evaluation procedures important to the writing process.

Computer-assisted composing offers many possibilities for enhancing the cognitive and metacognitive processes of students as they engage in the writing process. If used discriminately and tailored to the learning style of the students, computer writing tools can guide students "cognitively" as they improve their composition skills. The characteristics of skilled writers serve as a reference point or benchmark when evaluating the skills of adolescent writers. It is valuable to know how skilled writers approach writing tasks to assess the cognitive and metacognitive attributes of student writers. By identifying where students are in regard to the development of writing processes, we can also ascertain how far they need to go to become proficient writers, able to communicate clearly and effectively.

Composing requires a variety of planning, production, and revision processes that are recursive, interdependent, and interactive. Skilled writers engage in a number of cognitive activities as they compose. For example, they select and allocate specific strategies for writing. They also make easy transitions among the various writing processes by shifting their attention at any time throughout the writing process and by adjusting their awareness level to the task. Generally, good writers respond automatically to demands at the word or sentence level. Their awareness level increases as the task requirements become more complex, abstract, and meaning-based, necessitating more conscious consideration of the writing problem. Another characteristic of skilled writers is their ability to operate at several levels of awareness simultaneously. It is possible for most skilled writers to engage in subconscious self-monitoring as words are put on paper while consciously planning what to write next. Instructors should reinforce and build upon students' effective skills and strategies while providing new tactics and approaches to writing.

When students are first introduced to computer-assisted composing, they should be taught keyboard skills. Keyboard tutorials help avoid frustration for students as they learn other computer-composing skills. Most students learn the keyboard as well as numerous word processing commands in minimal time and can therefore avoid the "hunt and peck" method of typing that is both time-consuming and distracting to the beginning computer writer. After students feel comfortable with this new mode of writing, computer tools to facilitate writing processes can be introduced. Instruction in planning, production, and revision is important to the eventual integration of these writing processes.

Planning Processes

Students should be instructed in goal-related planning, which is an essential component of good writing (Scardamalia and Bereiter, 1986). Activating the knowledge that students have is a necessary part of the writing process. Students at the secondary level need a variety of memory strategies and procedural supports to help them gain access to knowledge and generate content. There is evidence that a combination of procedural facilitation of planning and substantive facilitation of content generation provides the necessary supportive base for the development of higher-level composing strategies (Scardamalia and Bereiter, 1986).

Computer-assisting composing software offers a variety of facilitative features to assist in goal-setting and composition planning. As an example, Wordbench, an integrated writing program published by Addison-Wesley, includes a subprogram called Brainstormer. This "add-in" program has a goal-setting feature that helps a writer define a subject, audience, point of view, and purpose. Another feature, Notetaker, allows the writer to jot down and organize ideas, facts, and information throughout the composition process. Good writers have a repertoire of strategies, such as taking notes, that enable them to store and organize ideas for later use. Outliners, a component of most integrated writing software, assist writers in organization of ideas and information by highlighting both primary and secondary composition goals. Most integrated programs incorporate some type of outliner. Chapter Three provided a review of several integrated composing programs that have components specifically designed to facilitate planning processes.

Another technique proven beneficial to writers during the early stages of writing is "assisted monologues," described by Scardamalia and Bereiter (1986) as a prompting approach wherein the student talks while the teacher inserts prompts to stimulate and enhance idea processing. This form of writing assistance is an integral part of writing process instruction. Conferencing, a type of assisted monologue, is a highly recommended aspect of composition instruction for secondary students. Two primary goals of writing conferences are the adoption of both cognitive and metacognitive strategies necessary for the production of written text and the internalization of writing processes associated with all phases of production. If the interaction during the writing conference is skillfully managed by the teacher, it can provide both substantive and procedural facilitation for the developing writer.

Computer prompting programs were among the first adaptations of on-line substantive facilitation techniques (H. Burns, 1984). These programs are useful throughout the writing process as an aid to planning, writing, or revising compositions and take the form of checklists to follow, lists of questions to answer, or self-generated questions and comments. Most prewriting programs follow the question-answer format as a way to activate students' knowledge and involve them in their writing. Mindscape's Prewrite 2, for instance, is designed as a first step in the writing process and, quite literally, has no commands, a feature that allows the program to be used by both experienced and inexperienced computer writers. This program helps writers overcome writing blocks and develop ideas by asking a series of questions as the student produces what is considered to be a rough set of notes to aid in the eventual development of an outline and composition. An added advantage of this program is its ability to modify, add, or delete questions; turn questions on or off depending upon the ability level of the student; or change and restore examples that accompany the questions. The teacher can modify the program at any time and monitor student files as they are created.

Many computer writing programs are based on a "boiler-plate" idea and offer frames and formats for producing specific types of writing. These writing supports are useful during composition planning particularly for students who have difficulty recalling discourse forms and knowledge. They also encourage collaboration and interaction among peers. Genre formats are available for both prose and verse. Formats are available for short stories, novels, personal narratives, persuasive essays, poetry, business letters, news stories, and research reports. Frames for bibliographic entries and footnotes are helpful for secondary students as they learn how to write a research paper. Students learn to develop annotated bibliographies and databases to share with others as they engage in cooperative or group writing projects.

Production Processes

The primary goal for writing instruction at the secondary level should be the development of a knowledge-transformation approach to composition (Bereiter and Scardamalia, 1987). This entails a shift from the immature knowledge-telling strategy to a mature model of composing, where the writer approaches writing as a problem to be solved. Knowledge transformation is a higher-order approach to writing. Using this approach, writers appropriate executive processes as they conduct memory searches and construct mental representations of text structure and content.

Bereiter and Scardamalia (1987) identified five essential goals of writing instruction that apply to secondary level writers:

1. Make students aware of all facets of the composing process.

2. Provide the necessary models for the problem-solving processes as they apply to writing.

3. Help students become aware of their own knowledge and cognitive processes as they write and continue to aim for higher competence levels.

4. Assist students in the development of challenging writing goals.

5. Use procedural supports to facilitate their acquisition of more complex executive processes.

Computer writing tools provide the kinds of supports necessary to achieve these instructional goals. Integrated writing programs, for example, can be used to increase awareness of the various dimensions of the composing process and their interactions. Metacognitive cues and prompts are embedded in many of these programs to enhance the development of executive or control processes and to increase both quantity and quality of text production. Production cues and signals assist writers in making smooth transitions from one idea to another and in making additions that integrate well into previously written material. Interactive computer prompting programs, such as Daiute's (1985b) CATCH, can help writers reconstruct and summarize what they have written to ensure that the added text fits with the original premise of the composition. These summaries can be written and reviewed easily by using the window feature of word processing programs. The window feature also permits students to refer to notes, information, outlines, diagrams, and references as they produce text.

An important characteristic of older writers is their ability to select appropriate strategies to locate information and construct knowledge from either internal or external sources and, later, to identify what they have learned from writing. They also have the ability to shift from higher-level to lower-level processes depending on the task demands and constraints. Mature writers show an awareness of and ability to write within constraints such as type of audience, composition length, production time, and adherence to genre and topic. Computer writing supports help students not only identify and acknowledge various constraints in writing, but also reduce the mechanical as well as deeper level demands placed upon them during the writing process. The next section on revision processes addresses the increased demands placed on the maturing writer.

Revision Processes

Scardamalia and Bereiter (1986) refer to revision as a special kind of reprocessing, which involves the transformation rather than substitution or addition of text. Reprocessing spans all aspects of writing from editing mechanical errors to reformulating goals. Viewed from a reprocessing perspective, revision can be either surface level, pertaining to word and sentence level modifications and transformations, or deep level, tending more toward concept and idea transformation. Additionally, revision can be either internal, taking place within the mind of the writer before the text actually is produced, or external, where the writer is required to read through the text and detect writing errors and inconsistencies in content. One goal of proficient writing is the automatization of surface level editing procedures, such as detection and correction of spelling and punctuation errors. This level of response frees the writer to concentrate on substantive revision by reducing the cognitive load due to concern for correctness and form. Computerized text editing and text analysis tools are indispensable for surface level revision. Spelling checkers and thesauruses are important tools to the writer who cannot afford to stop in midsentence to make corrections during composing. These interruptions are distracting and often cause writers to lose their train of thought. Computer tools enable writers to delay error correction until a draft is completed. This capability has helped low-achieving and reluctant writers to write more and take more pride in their writing (Rosenbaum, 1984).

A number of different style revision programs are available for deeper level revision. These programs identify patterns in writing, such as inflected forms of the verb "to be," passive voice constructions, nominalizations, vague or overused words, verbosity, sexist language, or confused homophones (Kiefer, 1987). Adolescent writers can use these programs as they develop, experiment with, and refine their writing styles. Computer prompting programs for revision use questions and comments, much like their companion programs for planning, to help students identify structural and contextual problems and select strategies to address these problems. These programs also promote metacognitive activities such as self-evaluation and self-monitoring by encouraging students, often in cooperation with peers and teachers, to evaluate their text structure and content and follow recommended guidelines for concept and idea level revision. Students need instruction in computer revision procedures and need to be guided through the revision process by the teacher. Collaborative editing and content revision is helpful to adolescent writers who need regular and substantive feedback as they become more confident and experienced with writing processes. A computer writing environment can provide many opportunities for this type of collaboration and cooperation among students as they perfect their composition skills.

Computer Writing Environment

A computer writing environment has several advantages over traditional classrooms for teaching writing processes to secondary students (Daiute, 1985b). In this environment, writing is more personal. Students are involved at a level where they do more than simply write a composition and submit it to their teacher to "correct" and grade. The writing curriculum characteristically is student centered, and instruction often is individualized. Students are given many more opportunities to practice all phases of the writing process. Computer-assisted composing encourages students to actively participate in the writing experience. They are encouraged to plan prior to producing text and revise, format, and edit compositions throughout the draft process. Nash and Schwartz (1987) preferred a computer environment for writing over other settings because it was found to reduce anxiety and free writers to take risks; help writers avoid writing blocks by alleviating many of their concerns about form, style, and mechanical errors; facilitate both surface and deep level revisions; create student-centered error analysis; and foster collaborative settings in which students and teachers confer on a continuing basis about works-in-progress. Several methods particularly conducive to writing instruction within a computer environment have been explored in secondary settings. These include conference teaching, collaborative learning, journal writing, and "I-Searching," which is a form of research writing (Rodrigues and Rodrigues, 1986).

Computer conferences assist students in their analytic writing by providing many opportunities to explore alternatives in their writing (Daiute, 1985b). Although conferences can take many forms, the workshop method seems to work well in writing laboratories. Here, the teacher circulates among students as they compose. Observation of students provides information to be used during more formal individual or group computer conferences. This type of conference promotes three-way interaction among students, teachers, and computers and gives students an opportunity not only to experiment with revisions, but also to discuss the pros and cons of changes with teachers and peers. Shared diskettes is another way to encourage interaction among students about their writing. These diskettes can be used simply to accumulate ideas, information, and points of view or can be used to make comments, pose questions, or provide other types of feedback to writers. Larger group conferences can be organized around a demonstration screen. Using this conference technique, teachers can model writing processes or demonstrate computer tools using actual drafts of students' compositions.

Electronic networks, or E-mail, is still another form of conference. This makes possible ongoing correspondence among students and encourages meaningful discourse, peer critiques, electronic "tutoring," and other types of communication among students and teachers (Kinkead, 1987). One popular use of networks is electronic journal writing, which is used to record ideas for essays, enter notes for courses, summarize and respond to reading completed in subject area classes, and write personal anecdotes and messages (Rodrigues and Rodrigues, 1986). Students should be taught how to organize their journal on separate files, which can be printed whenever a copy is needed. Messages or writing intended for others can be copied onto additional disks and then "sent" to students and teachers on the local or distance network who may respond directly on the disk.

Helen Schwartz's (1984) three-part program SEEN (the Seeing Eye Elephant Network) is an example of a collaborative electronic network for writing. In the first part of the program, students create hypotheses for their essays, provide supportive details, and consider alternatives and exceptions. A pen name is used when the student posts the work-in-progress as a "notice" on the network, which is essentially a public forum for comments and constructive criticism by students on one another's writing. The individual student's "notices" and comments about them are stored on the computer text file. The text file can be printed or loaded onto the word processor when the student wishes to continue writing. Students receive feedback and support for their writing from the moment ideas are conceived and articulated. Collaborative writing of this sort becomes an integral part of the computer writing environment and fosters cooperation and sharing among students as they learn and practice new writing skills.

Research report writing generally is a requirement in high school language arts classes. The I-Search method is a technique of research writing that encourages students to choose topics based on their interests and needs, learn all they can about the topic, and then present the results of their investigation (Macrorie, 1980; Rodrigues and Rodrigues, 1986). Microcomputers offer a host of computer tools such as subscription networks, idea processing programs, and sophisticated word processing programs to augment instruction in research methods and to facilitate the actual collection and integration of information. The computer writing environment at the secondary level should emphasize computer-based research skills associated with access to and creation of databases, organizing and storing data, and writing research reports. The teacher can use cooperative learning techniques to structure research assignments and further encourage interaction among students.

Conclusion

The developmental and psychological changes of adolescence combined with the more stringent academic expectations of secondary classrooms make it difficult for many students to succeed in school. Students are expected not only to have mastered basic academic skills, but also to have acquired a repertoire of cognitive and metacognitive strategies that enable them to effectively meet the academic challenges of the secondary classroom. Traditional writing instruction has been relatively unsuccessful in teaching the necessary writing processes and strategies that enable students to write competently at the secondary level. Research in writing process instruction as well as computer-assisted composing has indicated that the combination offers a promising alternative to current approaches to composition instruction. The computer writing environment provides a context where writing processes can be taught effectively and reinforced and where students become motivated and enthusiastic about writing.

CHAPTER 6

Computers and Writing with Special Needs Students

Special needs encompass a wide variety of learner differences including physical and sensory limitations, giftedness, learning disabilities, and cultural and linguistic differences. These differences often interfere with academic achievement and educational progress, particularly in a traditional classroom where a curriculum designed for "average" students is taught. The traditional classroom experience is ineffective for a large number of students who, to reach their potential, require adaptations of the curriculum and learning environment.

Dramatic changes have occurred in educational programs as a result of the passage of Public Laws 94-142, the Education for All Handicapped Children Act (1975), and 98-511, the Bilingual Education Act (1984). These two legislative acts mandated the accommodation of variation in learning ability and style in educational settings and implementation of instructional alternatives for students with special needs. Following the passage of the Education for All Handicapped Children Act, states receiving federal funds were required to provide free and appropriate educational programs for all children with handicapping conditions, regardless of type or severity. As a result of this mandate, children with learning disabilities, emotional problems, communication disorders, sensory impairments, mental handicaps, physical disabilities, or other conditions that may interfere with learning are evaluated and provided with educational programs designed to meet their special learning needs. Another component of the law mandated that handicapped children be educated in the "least restrictive environment." This regulation has to do with the concept of mainstreaming, which means that, "to the maximum extent possible," handicapped children must be educated with their nonhandicapped peers.

Culturally and linguistically different children represent another challenge to educational planners. The extent of this challenge is reflected by the Los Angeles School District, where over eighty different languages are spoken by school children. These children, who have been designated as Limited English Proficient (LEP), encounter problems in learning primarily as a consequence of their language difference. These learning problems typically stem from lack of instruction in the student's dominant language.

Programming for variation in intellectual ability, physical capability, learning style, interest, achievement level, and cultural and linguistic background of learners represents a significant problem for educators. Computers and other technological adaptations offer promising instructional alternatives for addressing the heterogeneity of students. Although the advantages of using computers in the classroom have been discussed in previous chapters, it is important to reiterate several of these in a discussion of students with special needs to identify features of computer-assisted instruction that are most salient for this disparate population.

The first, and perhaps most important, reason for using computers with special needs students is their capability to motivate and actively engage students in learning (Hoffman, 1983). Second, both individual and group instruction can be managed easily with computers. This feature simplifies coordination of lessons and activities and makes it possible to provide instruction that is interactive as well as individualized. Computers have the capability to interact directly with learners and provide ongoing and immediate feedback and reinforcement. A third advantage has to do with the flexibility of computers for educational planning. Numerous instructional variables including level of difficulty, presentation of material, reinforcement schedule, and type of computer-student interaction can be modified easily for individual learners. The flexibility associated with computer-based instruction represents a unique advantage over other modes of instruction when programming for learners with special needs (Anderson, 1982; Behrmann, 1984).

A fourth advantage of computers is their ability to wait for input and responses, allowing individuals control over their instructional pace and reinforcement schedule. Finally, a most appealing advantage is the ability of teachers to maintain detailed data about a learner's performance. Information about students can be collected, analyzed, and stored to assist with program evaluation and modification. This represents another distinct advantage for teachers who are responsible for educational planning for students with exceptionalities or special learning needs (Behrmann, 1984).

MacArthur (1988) delineated several word processing functions that seem to have a positive impact on the development of writers with special needs. These include the computer's capability to:

1. Reduce the physical demands of writing by replacing handwriting with typing.

2. Change the social context of writing by encouraging collaboration on writing projects and publication for a variety of audiences.

3. Promote interaction among teachers, students, and computers throughout the writing process.

4. Enhance writing strategy development by using interactive prompting programs.

6. Augment reading and writing activities with synthesized speech attachments.

7. Facilitate revision by using spelling and style checkers.

How computers can facilitate the writing process for students with learning disabilities, sensory impairments, physical disabilities, and linguistic differences is addressed in this chapter. Research in computer-assisted composing for these learners will be reviewed and recommendations given for adapting computer writing instruction to meet the special needs of learners.

Learning Disabilities

Learning disabilities encompass a range of developmental and learning problems that most often are associated with language and perceptual-motor difficulties, academic under-achievement, and social maladjustment. According to the definition contained in P.L. 94-142 (Education for All Handi-capped Children Act, 1975), a learning disability is a "disorder in one or more of the basic psychological processes involved in understanding or in using language, spoken or written, which disorder may manifest itself in an imperfect ability to listen, speak, read, write, spell, or to do mathematical calculations." Although students with other disabilities such as sensory impairment or mental handicaps also can manifest learning disabilities, they are excluded from the definition: "Such term does not include children who have learning problems which are primarily the result of visual, hearing, or motor handicaps, of mental retardation, of emotional disturbance, or of environ-mental, cultural, or economic disadvantage."

Students who have been identified as learning disabled generally have average or above average intellectual ability, but exhibit a significant discrepancy between their ability and achievement in school. Reading and writing disabilities are characteristic of many students who, as a result, find school-related tasks and academic learning particularly frustrat-ing and unpleasant. These students typically receive a portion of their instruction in special resource classes provided by teachers who have been trained in specific techniques and procedures for this population of learners. Characteristics of students with learning disabilities that may adversely affect their writing performance include:

1. Visual perception and perceptual-motor problems that interfere with recognition, recall, or production of letters and words.

2. Disorders in attention or the capacity to focus and sustain attention on a specific task.

3. Memory disorders or the ability to recall information and experiences.

4. Receptive and expressive language disorders.

5. Information processing problems related to the cognitive operations of concept formation, organization, and association.

6. Problem-solving difficulties.

7. Metacognitive problems that interfere with self-regulation and self-monitoring operations.

Morocco and Neuman (1986) cited further examples of problems that learning disabled children encounter when they write. Their observations of learning disabled students indicated weaknesses in the following areas: planning processes, which included topic selection, idea formation, and generation of supporting information; translation of thoughts into writing; ability to sequence narrative events; a general paucity of ideas for writing; knowledge and use of writing conventions such as conjunctions and transition words; spelling and punctuation; and attitude toward and confidence in their writing. The writing performance of students who have been identified as learning disabled may vary considerably due to the heterogeneity of this group and the diversity of characteristics associated with the condition. As a regular or special educator responsible for the education of youngsters with learning problems, it is critical not only to draw from a repertoire of instructional strategies and alternatives, but also to have available resources for adapting methods and materials. Computer-assisted composing provides extensive opportunities for adapting and tailoring instruction to meet the individual needs and enhance the writing of learning disabled students.

Related Research

Computer-assisted composing for learning disabled students is promising primarily in that it offers an array of alternatives to traditional writing instruction. The traditional approach has proved ineffective for most students with writing disabilities (Graham and Harris, 1988; Harris and Graham, 1988). Because research results generally have not indicated significant qualitative differences between compositions using word processing and those done with pencil and paper for this population of students, there has been some discussion regarding the usefulness of computer writing for them. In their discussion of the effects of word processing on the writing performance of learning disabled students, Goldman and Pellegrino (1987) offered an explanation for the limited effects on quality of writing commonly found in computer writing studies with these students. They suggested that the lack of "cognitive-academic" benefit might be attributable to students' poorly developed metacognitive skills and increased cognitive demands associated with using the keyboard.

Results of computer-assisted composing studies with under-achieving students generally are consistent with results of similar investigations with average and above average achieving students. It may be that simply providing students with word processing is not sufficient to produce substantial changes in quality of writing. Students, particularly those with learning problems, may need prior instruction in keyboard skills and selected software in addition to writing process instruction to improve quality of writing.

Empirical support is accumulating for using computer-assisted composing as an alternative mode of instruction with learning disabled students. In a study of the writing skills of fourteen learning disabled fourth graders, Morocco and Neuman (1986) made eighty-five observations of students writing with paper and pencil and the computer. Using a variety of outcome measures, they found that after using a word processor students were more willing to take risks and to persevere in their writing and appeared to enjoy the writing process more than they had with pencil and paper. Their major argument for using word processors with learning disabled children, however, has to do with the accessibility teachers have to students' writing processes during planning, production, and editing of compositions. The visibility of computer writing encourages spontaneous and frequent interaction and discussion among students and teachers. Teachers can stimulate students' thinking and writing and encourage internalization of writing processes through collaborative brainstorming, guided instruction, and feedback. It is necessary for teachers to become attuned to process instruction and not impose ideas and preferences on students or focus prematurely on formatting and mechanics. Because of their inaccurate and slow writing, students with poor skills are particularly vulnerable to "intrusions" by teachers. To guard against this, Morocco and Neuman (1986) recommended that teachers emphasize and promote students' ownership and control over their writing. Instruction in self-management and self-regulation strategies helps students assume responsibility for their academic performance. Students should be taught how to apply these metacognitive strategies to the composition process.

In another computer writing study with learning disabled fifth-graders, Jacobi (1986) found improvements in quantity of students' writing and the ability to detect and correct mechanical and spelling errors. The author also observed improved confidence and pride in writing as well as improved attitudes toward writing. Low self-esteem, motivation, and lack of confidence represent seemingly insurmountable barriers to learning for many students with learning disabilities. Early in the writing experience, positive changes in the affective domain can be as important as changes in academic performance.

Improvements in skills relating to language and writing were noted in word processing studies with learning disabled intermediate level students (Kerchner and Kistinger, 1984) and middle school students (Pernia, 1988; Shinn, 1987). Pernia's findings indicated that students who received instruction in word processing skills plus instruction in the practical application of these skills in the classroom outperformed students who received only word processing instruction. Performance was measured by the vocabulary, thematic maturity, and word usage subtests of the *Test of Written Language* (Hammill and Larsen, 1978). Using the same instrument, Kerchner and Kistinger (1984) measured writing performance differences between a group of students who were provided with a combination of writing process instruction and word processing and a control group. They found significant pre- and posttest differences favoring the experimental group on thematic maturity, word usage, style, and overall writing performance. Their results suggested that writing skills learned on the computer may effectively transfer to pencil and paper writing tasks.

Researchers at the Institute for the Study of Exceptional Children and Youth at the University of Maryland are responsible for much of the information to date on the effects of computer-assisted composing on the writing of students with learning disabilities. In one study of eleven learning disabled sixth graders, the production methods of handwriting, dictation, and word processing were compared (MacArthur and Graham, 1987). In this study, students who had considerable experience using a word processor were first interviewed about their writing and then asked to compose one story per week using each composition method. Dictated stories were found to be significantly longer, of higher quality, and grammatically more correct than either handwritten or word-processed stories. The only differences noted between the handwritten and word-processed stories were in composing rate and number of revisions. Production was faster and more revision between drafts was evident for the handwriting mode, whereas more revision occurred during the first draft of a composition produced using the word processor.

Another study by these authors (Graham and MacArthur, 1988) addressing metacognitive aspects of writing sought to determine the effects of self-instructional strategy training on students' production and revising processes. The researchers taught a sixth grader and two fifth graders a self-instructional strategy for generating and revising essays. Positive effects were noted for all students in revision, length, and quality of the compositions. Students maintained use of the strategy over time and transferred its use to a pencil and paper task. The self-instructional strategy enabled students not only to find and correct mechanical errors, but also to improve the clarity and cohesiveness of their compositions. If this capability can be paired with students' demonstrated ability to use the text-editing features of a word processor (MacArthur and Graham, 1987), it may be possible to substantially improve the quality of writing by learning disabled students. Emerging from research with these students are promising instructional alternatives to current practice in composition instruction.

Instructional Adaptations and Strategies

Both controlled and informal observations of learning disabled students as they compose on a computer support the need for instruction in keyboarding skills, word processing software, writing processes, and metacognitive strategies. Typically, students with learning disabilities require adaptations of strategies and techniques that have demonstrated effectiveness with normally achieving students. Principles and instructional procedures associated with direct instruction and behavioral interventions generally are recommended for learning disabled students, particularly during acquisition of new skills and knowledge. Modeling, verbalization, corrective feedback, reinforcement, and distributed practice are associated with effective instruction for these students. Additionally, it is often necessary to modify the task or the environment to accommodate the learning disabilities of students.

As their two-year study of word processing with learning disabled fourth graders progressed, Morocco and Neuman (1986) discovered that the computer changed the demands on students' knowledge and skill with regard to the machine itself, the environment, and the writing process. They discussed the need to increase learning disabled students' procedural knowledge in these areas when the computer initially is introduced into the classroom. Machine knowledge includes knowing how to load the word-processing software and data files, move the cursor and manipulate text, manage text, and discover errors in using the machine or software. Knowledge of the environment has to do with negotiating transitions between computer work and other classroom activities, successfully getting help when it is needed, and appropriately providing assistance to other students who may request it. Finally, knowledge of the writing process involves selecting an interesting topic, activating prior knowledge, having conferences with other students and the teacher, and acquiring review and revision skills. To avoid the pitfalls associated with the lack of keyboard and machine skills, Morocco and Neuman advocated teaching students a basic level of machine skills before having them use the computer to compose. Large screens can be used for demonstrations and hands-on exercises as students learn function keys and practice word processing commands. This activity seems to promote each transition to later composing activities. Another technique, in which pairs of students are provided with cue cards for prompting one another, also seems to support acquisition and application of writing skills. Although learning disabled students appear to improve in writing when they use these techniques, they frequently lack other skills necessary to fully participate in the learning process. Because of their lack of self-direction and interaction skills, these students usually need instruction in procedures for working both independently and cooperatively within the computer writing environment.

Manuals that accompany word processing programs may need to be adapted for learning disabled secondary and college students who must learn to independently read and understand directions for using software. Several excellent guidelines have been suggested for writing or rewriting instructions for word processing software (Collins, 1986, p. 51). These guidelines also are useful for adapting materials for younger students.

1. Instructions should be as brief as possible.

2. The layout should use spatial configurations and highlighting to enhance readability.

3. Key concepts and terms should be repeated.

4. Only information needed for the targeted level of use should be included.

5. Only one piece of information should be presented at a time.

6. Unnecessary computer jargon should be avoided.

7. Simple sentences should be used to isolate the term, operation, or concept being presented.

8. The text should be supported with clear diagrams.

9. Clear examples for each major term or operation should be provided.

10. Practice to reinforce new material must be embedded in the instructional routine.

Instructional programs for teaching learning disabled students how to compose on a computer should be developed with consideration for the needs of the individual student. A focus on individual needs improves the likelihood that students will benefit from instruction and begin to experience the pleasure of computer writing. Occasionally, students with severe motor coordination difficulties or reading disabilities will need additional assistance in the form of technological aids and supports such as keyboard alternatives and synthetic speech. Teachers are encouraged to be creative and use these devices as alternative writing tools for learning disabled students who may need them.

Physical and Sensory Impairments

The degree of a disability determines the level of support needed for success in school. Physical or sensory impairments create academic and social barriers for students that many times are overcome only with considerable adaptation of the educational program and learning environment. Compensatory programming for students with mild to severe physical and sensory disabilities has been revolutionized with the introduction of computers and technological aids into the schools.

Meyers (1984) enhanced both oral and written communication skills for children and adolescents with severe physical handicaps, visual handicaps, and cerebral palsy. She provided students with supportive computer tools to extend their skills and complete tasks not otherwise possible. This instructional program incorporated several of Papert's (1980) principles. The first of these, the *continuity principle,* requires a task to be continuous with previous experience and established personal knowledge. The second, termed the *power principle,* is based on the premise that interventions must empower learners as they become personally involved in learning activities. The third principle, *cultural resonance,* requires educational innovators to be sensitive to cultural values and use dynamic cultural trends to carry out educational interventions. Computer-based interventions for writing have opened a communication network enabling individuals who have limited communication options the opportunity to communicate with family members, teachers, peers, and others in school and the community.

Physical Disabilities

Physical disabilities describe a range of conditions such as cerebral palsy, muscular dystrophy, or spinal cord injuries that, to some degree, limit use of one's body and significantly interfere with participation in routine school or home activities. Academic learning frequently is difficult for students with orthopedic or other physical disabilities as a result of physical restrictions. Finding avenues of expression for students whose oral language is limited by physical problems is frustrating for teachers, parents, and students alike. Many students with physical disabilities experience problems not only in oral communication, but also in school-related tasks requiring written expression.

Several adaptive devices are available to help students with physical handicaps communicate through writing. By using whatever movement capabilities the student has, these adaptive devices allow the computer to interact with the student and facilitate communication in a variety of ways. Interactive computer techniques, classified as direct selection, scanning, and encoding, enable physically handicapped students to circumvent their disabilities and communicate effectively with other individuals (Candler, 1987).

Direct selection entails using a body part such as a finger, head, or arm to control some type of pointing device for assistance in typing on the computer keyboard. Keyguards, which are keyboard covers with holes for individual keys, accommodate individuals with limited typing ability. Users can rest their hands on the keyboard or move around the keyboard without unintentionally hitting keys. *Encoding,* a second method of computer interaction, provides computer accessibility through a code system transmitted by a switch or push-button device to assist persons whose movements are limited. A third interactive computer technique, termed *scanning,* allows individuals to use switches to activate a systematic computer search for an item. Either linear or row-column scanning patterns can be used to locate and activate keys. Adaptive devices are extremely sensitive and can be activated by minimal head movements or even eyebrow lifts. The Brow Wrinkle Switch, composed of a tiny lever that extends from a small box, is attached to a person's head with the lever resting just above the eyebrow. Movement of the eyebrow activates the computer to begin its search either by registering with the computer entry terminal or through some alternate communication aid. When the correct key is found, a second movement terminates the search while a third movement registers the selection. TETRAscan II, another adaptive communication aid, consists of a keyboard simulator that attaches to a standard computer. Composed of a keyboard and an interface unit, the simulator allows access to all keys on a regular keyboard and accommodates most available software. TETRAscan II is equipped with an electronic keyboard designed for ease of key selection and has several options for scanning and key selection that can be adapted easily to a user's needs. It also has memory capability to allow use of word and phrase shortcuts as the user composes messages, letters, or essays.

Visual Handicaps

A person is handicapped whose visual impairment "interferes with his or her optimal learning and achievement, unless adaptations are made in the methods of presenting learning experiences, the nature of the materials used, and/or the learning environment" (Barraga, 1983, p. 25). According to P.L. 94-142, "visually handicapped means a visual impairment which, even with correction, adversely affects a child's educational performance. The term includes both partially seeing and blind children."

The range of computer options and technological supports available for visually handicapped individuals makes it possible to meet the reading and writing needs of both partially seeing and totally blind individuals (Candler, 1987). Depending on the extent of their visual impairment, many partially seeing individuals can be accommodated by using large print software or computers that expand print from two to sixteen times its original size. The Large Print Computer, for example, a standard computer operated by a set of switches and a joystick, allows selection of print size as well as selection of rate and manner of print presentation. Another mechanism, Visualtek, enlarges letters up to 5½ inches tall on a monitor.

Auditory output is another option for visually impaired persons. Several different speech synthesizers are available to computer users who require auditory feedback in addition to the more customary visual feedback from the computer. These devices are available as complete packages, such as Information Thru Speech, or as attachments to standard computer systems. Computer speech synthesis enables students to hear words as they are typed and also listen to an entire document after it is completed. This option simplifies writing review and revision for visually handicapped students. Speech synthesis attachments such as ECHO+, Echo II, Cricket, or Smooth Talker are used in conjunction with word processing programs. To illustrate, Echo+ has two cursors that operate simultaneously. The audio cursor reviews and "reads" what has been written, whereas the standard cursor is used in the ordinary manner. An additional word processing feature for visually handicapped writers is the capability to use either print or Braille output.

The Kurzweil Reading Machine, a scanning device, permits users to read any printed or typewritten material. Printed material, such as a newspaper or letter, can be "read" simply by placing the material face down on a glass plate and then pushing a button to activate the voice mechanism. Options include word reading or spelling and adjustment in rate, volume, and pitch. By connecting with other information processing systems, the Kurzweil can be used for both information input and output. VersaBraille II, for instance, can be linked with the Kurzweil for speech output. VersaBraille II operates as a word processing unit and offers options similar to other sophisticated word processing programs, but, instead of recording print, it records Braille information on disk.

Another device used to facilitate writing for visually impaired individuals is the Cranmer Modified Perkins Brailler. By itself, the Cranmer can be used simply as a Braille typewriter; however, interfaced with a computer and using appropriate software and a Braille Printer, it has capabilities similar to a typical word processing system. Designed for the Apple II+, IIe, and IIc computers, Braille-Edit provides both word processing and Braille translation and offers most word processing options. Information transmission for this device takes the form of auditory (voice synthesis), visual (standard print), and tactile (Braille) output. Adaptive devices such as the ones described here provide visually handicapped individuals with alternatives and supplements to conventional word processing. Students who use these technological alternatives for reading and writing will be able to communicate more effectively with others and participate more fully in school and community events.

Hearing Impairments

Educational adaptations for hearing impaired students are determined by the degree of hearing loss, which can range anywhere from a mild loss to profound deafness. According to P.L. 94-142, "deaf means a hearing impairment . . . so severe that the child is impaired in processing linguistic information through hearing, with or without amplification, which adversely affects educational performance," and "hard of hearing means a hearing impairment, whether permanent or fluctuating, which adversely affects . . . educational performance but which is not included under the definition of deaf."

Most conventional computer hardware and software can be used by hearing impaired individuals without modifications, as their use does not require auditory input or output. As a result of their disability, students with hearing impairments usually have a difficult time acquiring the conventions of spoken and written language. Consequently, their speech and written language patterns, including syntax, word usage, and spelling, may deviate considerably from standard form. One advantage of word processing programs for these students is the variety of add-on computer writing tools available to locate and correct mechanical errors and check spelling, grammar, and word usage. In one study with hearing impaired students in junior and senior high school, Brady and Dickson (1983) found that students seemed more motivated to write and improve their writing skills when using computers. These authors focused on referential communication skills in a cooperative situation with both hearing and hearing-handicapped peers. Students were required to describe one of a number of displayed visual foils that a second student was required to identify. As a result of this charade-type game, the level and duration of interaction and quality of communication among students increased.

Both Epstein (1986) and Lederer (1985) designed writing curricula for hearing impaired students around computers and writing process instruction. They suggested instructing students in the fundamentals of computers and keyboarding skills prior to the introduction of word processing software; requiring mastery of the most important functions of the program such as starting a file, inserting text, reading a menu, moving the cursor, adding and deleting text, and printing documents before making writing assignments; and having students of varying language levels work on assignments in dyads or small groups.

The telecommunication capabilities of computers also enable hearing impaired students to communicate more effectively and more frequently with other individuals, particularly with hearing persons. Both local and national communication networks allow students to send and receive mail electronically, post notices and messages on electronic bulletin boards, or actually converse with another person via the computer. This capability provides the opportunity for hearing impaired persons to converse and interact with persons for whom communication otherwise would be restricted or even impossible.

Cultural and Linguistic Differences

A component of educational programming for students whose primary language is other than English is instruction in

English as a second language (ESL). ESL classes typically focus on acquisition of vocabulary and syntax in English and on instruction in oral language, reading, and writing skills. Frequently, classes are composed of students whose cultural and linguistic backgrounds and levels of English competency vary substantially. By facilitating individualized instruction and by motivating students and encouraging their cooperation and interaction, computers can assist language-different learners in learning English. Word processing programs offer many options to the instructor for structuring the ESL program around the individual needs and language levels of the students and also offer options to students in regard to activities for acquiring, practicing, and applying both oral and written language skills (Huffman and Goldberg, 1987).

In her discussion of the value of word processors in ESL programs, Piper (1987) made the following suggestions and identified several reasons for using word processing with students who have limited English proficiency. As an instructional tool, she maintained, the word processor can be used to build vocabulary as students learn how to use both hardware and software. It also can be used to structure small-group work and foster conversation in English about oral and written language conventions. Activities or exercises should focus on learners' attention to features of the target language such as text structure or pronoun use. As a writing tool for students, the word processor can be used to produce writing that has a professional look and to detect and correct textual errors. Word processing for ESL students, as for other populations of learners, relieves the frustration of revising and rewriting text as the writer works toward a final draft. Thus, the word processor becomes the vehicle for moving from a first draft through corrections, deletions, and additions of material to a final draft that is acceptable to both writers and their teachers. As a result of these adaptations, students may concentrate more on their writing as they strive for perfection (Piper, 1987).

It seems likely that using a word processor as the vehicle for writing and the centerpiece for communicating about language forms and patterns will improve second language oral and written language skills for students. It also seems likely that computers and word processing will alleviate some of the problems associated with instructing students whose English skills are not at the level where they can profit from instruction in English. While working with Spanish-speaking first graders, Brisk (1985) observed that children who used computers to compose in Spanish changed in their perception of themselves as learners and in their attitudes and behaviors toward writing. The children became more fluent both in reading and writing, began to read for meaning, and developed a sense of text and audience in their writing. Brisk (1985) concluded that "the computer could be used to develop literacy among very young children regardless of their initial ability to read or write" (p. 31).

Summary

Computers are powerful tools for developing written language skills for students with special needs. This chapter focused on using computer-assisted composing to enhance learning and facilitate the writing process for students with learning disabilities, physical handicaps, visual and hearing impairments, and linguistic and cultural differences. Several benefits of using computers for writing instruction with special needs learners have been demonstrated. The research in computers and writing with these populations of students is encouraging and offers many possibilities for improving current instructional practice.

CHAPTER 7

Evaluation and Selection of Computer Writing Tools

Computer-assisted composing, like other forms of computer-assisted instruction, requires software appropriate to the age, developmental level, and instructional needs of learners. Many different computer writing tools to facilitate and augment the writing process have been described in previous chapters. Descriptions of hardware or software, however, do not provide sufficient information for educators who are responsible for recommending the purchase of materials and equipment for their schools' computer writing programs. Guidelines developed specifically for evaluating, comparing, and contrasting computer hardware and software are necessary in order to select the most appropriate tools for learners. With the proliferation of software in the area of writing and language arts, it is critical to establish criteria for evaluating the suitability of computer tools for teaching and learning composition skills. It also is essential that instructors become skilled in the evaluation and selection of computer writing tools to avoid the purchase of expensive equipment and materials that may be inappropriate for their students.

The Need to Evaluate Computer Writing Tools

Prior to selecting computer tools, teachers need to assess the writing skills of their students (Daiute, 1985b; MacArthur and Shneiderman, 1986). As discussed in previous chapters, students often have problems deciding what to write, organizing their ideas, generating sentences and paragraphs, and editing and revising text. Once strengths and weaknesses in these aspects of the writing process are detected, instructors can begin to tailor instruction to meet the students' needs. For example, certain students may excel in creative writing but have difficulty writing reports. Other students may have mastered many of the mechanical writing skills but lack the organizational skills needed for producing coherent text. After specific student strengths and weaknesses such as these have been noted, instructional methods and materials to address student attributes should be identified. In a computer writing environment, this includes matching students with computer writing tools appropriate to their instructional level and writing needs.

Individualized instructional programs can operate efficiently within the larger writing community. Computer writing groups or dyads use a peer tutoring model to group or pair students who have specific writing strengths with students who need assistance in certain aspects of writing. These instructional alternatives provide options to independent student writing and help accommodate varying abilities, achievement levels, and interests of students during writing activities.

Piper (1983) cited several reasons for evaluating software before using it with student writers. First, not all students are motivated to use the computer for writing, so some students may need introductory programs to increase their familiarity with computers and to illustrate how computers can be helpful in writing. Second, it is important to select software that complements writing process instruction and also facilitates students' transfer of acquired writing skills to compositions produced on the computer. A third consideration has to do with writing style and the ability to interact successfully with computers. Students who seem to be intimidated by the computer or whose writing may be inhibited as a result of using the computer may need gradual exposure to computer writing as well as graduated practice using a variety of computer writing tools.

Considerations for Selecting Computer Writing Tools

Before purchasing equipment and materials for a computer-assisted composing program, teachers and administrators also need to consider the number of students who will be using and sharing computers as well as their ages and developmental levels. Another important consideration is the amount of money available to purchase equipment and establish the computer writing environment. Budget constraints often are the determining factor in the design and character of a computer writing environment and instructional programs. Computer accessibility is a major concern for instructors because students require varying amounts of time on the computers as they acquire computer skills. Not only do students need time to learn how to use the hardware and software, they also need time to learn and practice new computer-based composing skills.

In his discussion of computers and writing instruction, Marcus (1987) identified three levels of student involvement and the implications of these levels of involvement for evaluating and selecting software. The first level of involvement consists essentially of encouraging students to use word processing for writing. There is little need to provide more than information about various types of word processing programs at this level. At the second level where class time is devoted to computer-assisted composing, computer lab teachers and consultants provide much of the information for program development and usually participate in decisions about hardware and software selection. The third level, in contrast to the others, involves a more diverse representation of educators, because at this level teachers across the disciplines design and lead their own workshops, create special writing assignment files, and use specialized software for addressing specific writing skills. Marcus maintained that regardless of the level at which educators choose to involve students, the following aspects of the program must be addressed:

1. Purpose and goals of the computer writing program.

2. Benefits, advantages, and disadvantages of using computer writing with students.

3. Hardware and software needs for establishing a program.

4. Facilities for the computer writing program.

5. Format of instruction.

6. Scheduling of classes and writing labs.

7. Abilities and needs of students.

Attention must be given to Marcus's levels of involvement and to the concerns associated with each level if a productive and effective writing environment is to be established and maintained.

Instructional Goals

Instructional goals and objectives should guide the selection of software for computer-assisted composing. Within the structure of the writing program, the teacher must decide if there is a need to provide specific instruction in prewriting and revision skills and, if so, whether instruction in these skills will be augmented by software designed specifically for such activities. Integrated software packages, such as QUILL and HBJ Writer, incorporate a variety of writing programs to enhance the basic word processing program that forms the core of these packages. However, if integrated software is too expensive or not available, writing instructors may need to build component programs to address specific composing needs of students that cannot be met simply with word processing software. Bankstreet III, for example, offers supplementary programs that interface with word processing software. These supplementary programs can be purchased separately and usually include a variety of writing activities focusing on different elements of the writing process.

To improve students' planning processes, for example, teachers may decide to use heuristic prompters, topic browsers, outlining functions, genre templates, or window functions.

These tools can be indispensable for individualizing student writing programs. After using such prewriting activities for planning compositions, students translate their ideas and thoughts into text that is linguistically and contextually acceptable. Phrase expanders and speech recognition programs offer exciting possibilities for improving the translation process. Although most of these options still are relatively expensive, it should not be long before prices are such that a variety of tools can be incorporated into the instructional program.

After expressing ideas in writing, students are required to review their compositions and make necessary revisions. During this phase of the writing process, students polish their writing by making both surface level and content revisions. Revising compositions frequently is the most problematic phase of the writing process for students. Revision processes may need to be directly taught and reinforced. Telecommunication networks can be used to provide review and feedback on students' writing. These networks provide the opportunity for students to interact about their writing with other students and their teachers. If computers are linked into a local or commercial network, it is possible to transmit students' compositions to anyone on the network. Teachers and students can evaluate and comment on compositions as they evolve.

Another breakthrough for text evaluation identified by Pea and Kurland (1987) entails reformatting text to simplify its reading. Grouping psycholinguistically defined "chunks" of text enables readers to read and remember text more easily. Text can be reformatted in a sentence-by-sentence or phrase-by-phrase format. Writers can also use large screens to see more text at one time. Grammar, spelling, and mechanical error detection is facilitated by using any number of text analysis programs designed for these purposes. Critical dialogue annotators, which log critical suggestions and questions posed by teachers and peer evaluators, and genre-specific style analyzers also are helpful in evaluating text.

Pea and Kurland (1987) noted that separation of the writing processes alleviates some of the cognitive burden of remembering the many goals associated with constructing compositions. Writing goals can be established ahead of time and monitored throughout the writing process by using various word processing options such as window functions and screen division. Care must be exercised in selecting computer tools to assist with writing subprocesses. Tools should be appropriate to the students' age and have features that are simple to understand and use. The caveat here is to ensure that all computer writing tools are previewed and evaluated carefully prior to implementation in the writing program. It is a good idea not only to have instructors try out the software, but also to have students use it on a trial basis and express their reactions regarding its suitability. In this way, its appropriateness for use with other students can be ascertained. A software review committee should be formed to assist in the evaluation process. This committee can establish software evaluation criteria that reflect both the writing needs of the students and the instructional goals of the writing program.

Hardware Selection

Before purchasing computers for a writing program, educators need to be cognizant of a number of important factors that help guide and facilitate the selection process. When purchasing educational computing systems, it is important to know what one is buying. Computer systems include a basic computer, plus a central processing system, memory, keyboard, input-output ports, and built-in programs. Most important, says Johnson (1986), is the system's capability of adding software and hardware peripherals to the basic computer that will permit teachers to implement educational programs in their classrooms. In other words, the computer system should be able to support the kinds of educational activities that make up the program. For example, a writing program may begin with only a simple word processing program, but eventually be expanded to include a variety of powerful writing tools and telecommunication components. A microcomputer can be transformed into a terminal for a mainframe or minicomputer by inserting a communications card, providing the connection to a modem. The modem, an acronym for modulator-demodulator, is a device that translates signals over communication or telephone lines to another modem, which is connected to a large-capacity computer. Information can be sent and received, enabling computer users to communicate with one another on a continuing basis. A communication network system is a very desirable component of a computer-assisted writing program because of the limitless opportunities to directly communicate with other writers and the easy access from virtually any setting connected to the system.

Computers should be purchased with consideration for their long-term benefits rather than to satisfy immediate needs. An educational plan should be developed that identifies both short- and long-term needs for the writing program. It may be that the design of the most powerful or most expensive computer will not meet the needs identified in a long-range plan. Because it is likely that the educational plan will include expansion over several years, only computers that can be upgraded to accommodate more powerful programs should be considered.

Another important consideration in hardware selection is the computer's software support capabilities and its ability to accommodate peripherals and adaptive devices. Computers should have interface capabilities, which means that circuitry cards can be inserted into the computer to update the linkage system or add peripherals to an existing system. The computer system's flexibility is as important as memory capacity and processing speed. Flexibility is of paramount concern when selecting a computer for educational computing, because fewer limitations mean greater opportunities for learners. To illustrate, alternatives to the traditional keyboard include such devices as joysticks, paddles, mice, and light pens. These devices have the potential to provide computer experiences for students whose physical restrictions might otherwise preclude computer use.

Cost is most definitely a factor and frequently determines the direction that educational programs take. When addressing computer program costs, it is necessary to keep in mind the long-range educational program goals. Is it better to purchase only one or two computers with features that complement the long-range goals of the educational computing program, or is it

Figure 7.1.

GUIDELINES FOR REVIEW AND EVALUATION OF ENGLISH LANGUAGE ARTS SOFTWARE

Compared with other educational media, instructional software is still in its very earliest stages of development. Developers and publishers of software are still learning how to best use the computer as a teaching medium. For this reason, the evaluation of software remains an imprecise process. Therefore, perhaps the best guidelines for evaluating software is to judge it against its producer's claims. That is, compare the product's performance against what the publisher claims it will do. Also, compare it against other products that attempt to teach the same concepts and skills. Finally, try to review a wide range of software and note how each uses the computer to present the instruction.

Guidelines for Software Review and Evaluation

Program: _____

Producer: _____

Required Equipment: _____

_____

Grade Level: _____ Cost: _____

Overall Program Objectives: _____

_____

Single Lesson Objectives
(if you are reviewing one lesson only):

Answer *yes* or *no* for the following criteria in Section I through V.

I. MANAGEMENT FEATURES

___ 1. Program provides teacher with a management system. (If no, go to Section II.)

___ 2. Program has record-keeping system that is useful and efficient.

___ 3. Records are easily retrievable.

___ 4. Teacher can assign or change performance levels and otherwise modify or add to records.

II. CONTENT

___ 1. Content is accurate.

___ 2. Content is appropriate to grade levels for which it is intended.

___ 3. Content can be modified by student or teacher.

___ 4. Possible content modifications are appropriate to the subject matter.

___ 5. Program can contribute integrally to the total English language arts curriculum.

___ 6. Program achieves its purpose.

___ 7. Program is likely to be motivating to students.

III. INSTRUCTIONAL STRATEGY

Note: If the software you are reviewing uses an instructional strategy other than tutorial or drill and practice, go to the Guidelines Addendum (Alternate Section III) to complete this section. Then continue with Section IV.

___ 1. Program is attractive.

___ 2. Program provides opportunity for practice.

___ 3. Practice is sufficient to help ensure mastery.

___ 4. Examples are provided.

___ 5. Examples are clear.

___ 6. Presentation is logical and well organized.

___ 7. Student has control over rate of presentation.

___ 8. Feedback for incorrect responses is helpful for discovering correct answers.

___ 9. Program allows learner to review, repeat, or advance according to performance.

___ 10. Program reports student performance periodically.

___ 11. Program provides an appropriate balance between content presentation and student interactions or responses.

___ 12. Program offers a variety of interactions, varying keys pressed or responses required.

___ 13. Program stimulates cognitive growth (or promotes thinking skills beyond recall of information).

___ 14. Program complements (or enhances) other English language arts materials.

___ 15. Program calls for meaningful application of English language arts skills.

IV. EASE OF OPERATION

___ 1. Directions to student are clear.

___ 2. Directions are accessible when needed.

___ 3. Student can operate program independently.

___ 4. Student is prevented from getting lost in the program, with no way out.

___ 5. Student is provided with option to quit or continue at any time.

V. SUPPLEMENTARY MATERIALS

___ 1. Program provides teacher's guide.

___ 2. Program provides supplementary student materials.

___ 3. If yes, materials are appropriate and useful.

___ 4. Program provides pre- and post-tests.

___ 5. Replacement print materials are available from producer.

Overall Evaluation

Use the scale at the right to rate this program. (1 is lowest; *NA* means *Not Applicable*.)

I. MANAGEMENT FEATURES	1 2 3 4 5 NA
II. CONTENT	1 2 3 4 5 NA
III. INSTRUCTIONAL STRATEGY	1 2 3 4 5 NA
IV. EASE OF OPERATION	1 2 3 4 5 NA
V. SUPPLEMENTARY MATERIALS ...	1 2 3 4 5 NA

SUMMARY COMMENTS
(Continue on back of sheet, if necessary.)

Program's Strengths and Weaknesses: _____

_____

_____

_____

_____

_____

Figure 7.1 *Continued*

Students' Responses to Program
(Briefly indicate number of students, grade levels, etc.): _____

_____
_____
_____

Recommendations:_____
_____
_____
_____

Guidelines Addendum
(Alternate Section III)

Choose the description which best fits the software you are reviewing, and respond to each criterion under that heading with a yes or no.

A. SIMULATION/PROBLEM-SOLVING
    (A program in which students learn through discovery and decision making)

____ 1. Problem-solving situation is realistic.
____ 2. Design is motivating.
____ 3. Procedural tasks are clearly sequenced.
____ 4. Feedback about user's decision is helpful.
____ 5. Suggestions are given for optimum performance.
____ 6. Outcomes or choices are explained.
____ 7. The program is relevant to the acquisition of English language arts skills.

(Go on to Section IV.)

B. EDUCATIONAL GAME

____ 1. Format is motivating..
____ 2. Graphics are appropriate to presentation.
____ 3. Content is relevant to English language arts skills.
____ 4. Learner has access to help or review.
____ 5. There is an appropriate reward for success and no "reward" for incorrect responses.
____ 6. Additional information or clues are provided by error feedback.

(Go on to Section IV.)

C. TEACHER UTILITY
    (A program which allows teacher to "author" the content within a programmed format)

____ 1. Directions to teacher are clear.
____ 2. Items are easy to enter.
____ 3. Editing is possible.
____ 4. Format for presenting items to student is appropriate.
____ 5. Student directions are clear.
____ 6. The type of interaction is appropriate to the skills taught.
____ 7. Record keeping capability is provided.

(Go on to Section IV.)

D. WORD PROCESSING/TEXT EDITING

1. **Management Features**

____ a. Utility functions (e.g., cataloging, renaming, protecting, deleting, copying files) are adequate.
____ b. Supplemental materials (such as summary command cards, worksheets, spelling checkers) are provided.
____ c. Editing utilities (e.g., capacity for adding words to spelling checkers) are adequate.
____ d. Management options (such as printing files) are available to and easy to use by students.

2. **Safeguards**

____ a. Directions or warnings at critical decision points (e.g., "Are you sure you want to delete this paragraph?") are given.
____ b. Back-up disks are available.
____ c. User can undo a previous action (e.g., return paragraph to its original position).

3. **Editing**

____ a. Formating features (e.g., upper/lower case, centering, underlining, tabs, subscripts) are adequate for intended audience and use.
____ b. Editing features (such as deletion and insertion of characters, words, paragraphs) are adequate for intended audience and use.
____ c. Command keys are logical and relatively easy to use.

4. **Visual Presentation**

____ a. Displayed characters are sufficiently readable for intended audience (e.g., 25, 40, 80 characters per line).
____ b. There is adequate space between lines or print.
____ c. Lines terminate at word boundaries.

5. **Printing**

____ a. Print formats (e.g., page width, page length, spacing) are flexible and adequate for intended audience and use.
____ b. The selected print format can be displayed on the screen prior to printing.

(Go on to Section IV.)

E. OTHER TYPES OF SOFTWARE

If the software you are reviewing does not fall into any of the above categories, you may wish to give a brief description of it below, followed by your evaluative comments.

_____
_____
_____
_____
_____
_____
_____
_____

(Go on to Section IV.)

Source: Prepared by the Committee on Instructional Technology, Reprinted with permission of the National Council of Teachers of English.

more advantageous to buy several computers to meet short-range program goals? Establishing computer writing labs may require concessions at the outset to get the type of equipment and program desired in the long run. Thus, it seems more important to start a program with only a few computers that can be upgraded as program goals are expanded rather than buy computers that could eventually restrict program development.

Selecting a printer for the writing program also is important. Because the quality of print and speed of printing can vary substantially, it is necessary to examine both of these attributes before purchasing printers. Dot-matrix printers, the least expensive type, form letters consisting of a series of dots, whereas letter-quality printers produce typewriter-quality text. Dot-matrix printers generally include a correspondence-quality option in addition to the data processing print option typical of earlier models. Printing speed is slower for correspondence quality, as the printer essentially prints over the regular dot-matrix print. Lesser quality dot-matrix print is fine for drafts, but for final copies of text it is desirable to have at least one letter-quality printer available to writers. Letter-quality printers are somewhat more expensive than dot-matrix models, but may be worth the additional expense, particularly if classroom publication is an integral part of the writing program. Even more expensive is the laser printer, which produces text that essentially is indistinguishable from typeset print. If funds are available, laser printers are ideal as part of a desk-top publishing program.

Software Selection

The Committee on Instructional Technology of the National Council of Teachers of English developed a set of criteria that may be used by educators at all levels to evaluate software for language arts instruction (NCTE, 1983). These generic evaluation criteria, reproduced in Figure 7.1, are useful for judging the effectiveness and value of word processing and other types of software programs for writing instruction. As part of the evaluation process, the committee suggested educators first become familiar with the evaluation guidelines to fully understand how the same categories can be used for evaluating different types of software. In addition to these generic categories, however, the guidelines include specific criteria for evaluating programs that differ from drill and practice or tutorial formats. Instructors should try out software before allowing student use. This preview permits the instructor to make informed observations of students' responses to the programs. Instructors are encouraged to look specifically for evidence that students are learning from the program and are actively involved and motivated. After progressing through these initial steps, the following features of software programs are evaluated:

1. Management capability.

2. Content of the program.

3. Instructional strategies.

4. Ease of operation.

5. Availability of supplementary materials.

The overall evaluation section of the guidelines provides the opportunity to rate each of these five features, write comments, and summarize the evaluations. Instructors then evaluate students' responses to the program and make recommendations as to how the software might be used within the context of the language arts program. Additionally, instructors are urged to judge the performance of the software against the producer's claims. This will help determine if it actually accomplishes what it is supposed to accomplish. At the same time, the teacher can compare it with other products that purport to teach similar skills and concepts.

Other researchers have expressed their concerns regarding writing software evaluation. In Marcus's (1987) view, one problem in evaluating software is that educators are not equipped to recognize good software when they see it. He poses the following four questions that underlie all software evaluation processes (p. 38):

1. To what degree does the software teach what it says it is supposed to teach?

2. How easy is it to learn, and how easy is it to use?

3. Will users need to provide their own instructions for learning the program?

4. Can users get most of what the program offers from a less expensive package?

According to Bork (1987), good software should hold the student's attention and adequately use the computer's interactive and individualizing capabilities. Educational objectives of the software should be easily ascertained. Heavily text-dependent or picture-dependent presentations must be avoided unless integral to the program. Instructions at the beginning of programs should be readily understood by both teachers and students, and programs should not rely on auxiliary print material for its effectiveness. Although generic criteria such as these are important when evaluating writing tools, specific attributes of word processing programs and augmentative computer writing software also should be considered. For this reason, evaluation techniques for word processing programs, keyboard tutorials, network systems, and supplementary writing tools are discussed separately.

Word Processing Programs

Choosing word processing software entails deciding whether to use what are considered to be age-appropriate programs with students or teach youngsters to use adult word processing programs. There are certain advantages and disadvantages to each choice (Knapp, 1986). Young children may adapt more easily to a simple package designed specifically for their age group than to a difficult, upper-level program. At some point, students will need to learn more advanced word processing programs because these are the programs generally found in homes and businesses. It may be appropriate to introduce more sophisticated programs earlier in the curriculum for capable students. Curriculum developers should make a decision regarding this issue. If age-appropriate software is selected for young writers, the curriculum should include a level system that incorporates transitions to more powerful and versatile word processing programs.

Piper (1983) advocated the use of simple, easy programs when students are initially exposed to word processing. Young and inexperienced students may profit from screen-directed programs that permit writers to consult the screen rather than the manual for program directions. Very young or reading disabled students will benefit more from screen directions that are in the form of pictographs or text-to-speech prompts. Readability of screen directions is as much a concern as readability of the manual. When students consult the manual, they must be able to read and comprehend directions as well as locate sections that relate directly to their questions. All too often manuals are written by computer experts who have no background in education and, consequently, do not consider the needs of learners as manuals are developed. The visual presentation of the screen also is a concern. Lines should be adequately separated by spaces, line length should be easily controlled, and a whole word should automatically move to the following line at the end of the screen instead of splitting inappropriately. This "wrap-around" feature is essential. In addition to these characteristics, text entry and edit features, formatting, file handling, printing, and several other features of word processing programs should be reviewed during the selection process (Batey and Ricketts, 1987; Knapp, 1986).

Text Entry and Edit Features. A single write-edit mode allows the writer to edit while writing rather than switching back and forth between the write and edit modes. Many programs provide the option of either inserting text or typing over existing text. An insert mode is essential, as typing over text automatically deletes characters as new text is typed. The insert mode allows writers to insert new text without simultaneously deleting what has been written. Cursor control is an important consideration in evaluating a program's editing characteristics. A writer should be able to move the cursor up, down, left, and right while moving through text as the place in the document is located. The delete function should enable writers to delete single letters, words, or sections of text. Most programs offer a block transfer function, whereby sentences, paragraphs, or larger sections of text can be marked, moved, copied, or deleted using only two or three commands. The search and replace function can be useful in automatically locating and changing a word throughout a document.

Formatting Text. Formatting text can be a problem unless the word processing program permits the writer to make such choices as the text is written and before it is printed. Embedded commands enable a writer to alter spacing, margins, and indentions, whereas format commands from a menu allow changes for the entire document. Various features such as line spacing, page numbering, underlining, boldfacing, and adjustable margins are desirable in word processing programs. Mnemonic codes that use simple associations to remember basic commands are helpful.

File Handling. Writers must be able to save their files on disk and also load a file that has been saved. This should be a simple process and easily learned by students, who then are responsible for their personal files. Students must become familiar with the save command to prevent loss of text. A built-in automatic save function can alleviate many of the problems associated with saving text and managing files. Writers should be taught at the outset how to create, save, edit, name, and print files. Understanding how filing systems work entails realizing that text stored in the computer memory is different from text stored on the disk (MacArthur and Shneiderman, 1986). The basic functions of the computer directly related to file management should be explained clearly to students before they begin using the word processor and then should be reviewed periodically to reinforce their understanding.

Printing a Document. Rather than always having to print an entire document, it is important to be able to print only one page or a section of text. The program should be able to stop printing at any time during the process. Before printing, the writer should be able to control such formatting aspects as centering, page numbering, margins, and spacing. It is easier for writers if the printer prints exactly what appears on the screen. This advantage generally is referred to as the *what you see is what you get* feature.

Support Features. Programs should come equipped with clear, comprehensive user manuals, quick reference guides that contain all the basic commands, help menus or screens that are easily used during text writing, and a good interactive, on-screen tutorial for teaching the fundamentals of the word processing program (Daiute, 1985b). Other helpful support materials include a teacher's guide to facilitate instruction for young writers and a set of activities or learning aids for students.

Miscellaneous Features. Having the option of both menu-driven and control-key commands for making selections is a convenience for users. To facilitate selection for very young or disabled writers, icons or graphic symbols, touch-sensitive screens, and peripherals such as the mouse or light pen are good supports. The ability to vary column size and alternate among them is important, particularly if the same program is used with different age groups of students. Screens may be divided into 20-, 40-, or 80-character columns, with the smaller column sizes yielding larger type. Entering "frozen" text to create prompted writing files for students can be a useful technique for teachers who wish to insert prompts in their writing lessons. However, it is a good idea to check that the prompts cannot be written over and also that they are not included in the printout of the document. Another useful feature is the file merger where a file can be attached to an already existing file.

Other Concerns. Other word processing features that should be considered include the amount of text the program can handle at one time, the program speed, and the variety and number of extra features such as multiple windows and formatting commands (Daiute, 1985b). Powerful word processing systems require relatively powerful computers. These, of course, cost more than less complex and less flexible systems. Perhaps the most important selection criterion for word processing programs is how easy they are to use. User-friendliness and the ease with which the program can be integrated into the writing program are eminently important when selecting writing software. Daiute (1985b) made several recommendations that should be considered when selecting writing tools for writers of different ages. For young writers from age four through approximately age eight, important features include on-screen formatting, a large character option, graphics editors, speech synthesis programs, light pens, and joysticks. Word processing recommendations for nine- to thirteen-year-old writers include an 80-column screen, upper and lower case letters, easy block moves, two-window features, and on-screen formatting commands. Adolescents seem to need both basic and advanced commands, allowance for documents longer than ten pages, a two-window feature, and a full set of formatting commands.

For students with special learning problems, other recommendations should be noted. In a study of upper elementary school learning disabled students taught to use a word processor, MacArthur and Shneiderman (1986) found the most persistent difficulties to be confusion about correct use of spaces and returns. Visible returns, an option on some word processing programs, may alleviate this problem by helping students to visualize the outcome and see the results of insertions and deletions more clearly. The ability to print the screen display eliminates this problem, but these authors correctly point out that word processing programs with this option generally are more costly and require an 80-column display. They also found that students with learning disabilities read monochrome displays more easily than they read color monitors.

Keyboard Tutorials

It generally is good practice to incorporate keyboard instruction into word processing instruction in order to avoid the formation of inefficient typing habits or reliance on a "hunt and peck" approach to keyboard use. Knapp (1986) developed a list of priorities for selecting a typing or keyboard tutorial. Her list of essentials include early introduction and illustrations of correct use of home keys, adequate practice lessons on frequently used letter and word combinations, and plenty of feedback to users concerning their accuracy and speed. Other important aspects include familiarization with both upper- and lower-case letters, error correction facility during exercises, and the ability to escape a lesson at any time and return to the previous menu without rebooting the system. Additionally, programs should provide space for teacher-developed lessons and tests and for students to establish goals and monitor their own progress. Tutorials should offer speed exercises, accuracy exercises, or a choice of the combination. Finally, programs should represent a variety of vocabulary levels suitable for different levels of learners and should focus on acquisition of typing skills rather than simply focus on increasing a user's speed.

Network Systems

Long-range plans for computer writing programs should include telecommunications networks. These allow users access to information utilities and databases and communication capabilities on local, national, or international networks. Subscriptions to services usually require an initial or yearly fee, connect-time fees, and a long distance telephone access code. Selecting an information utility like The Source or CompuServe requires the user to consider cost of the service, the type of people in the user community, and use-time (Daiute, 1985b). Utilities generally include such standard services as mail, chat, bulletin boards, word processing, news checks, and databases on a variety of topics. Access times vary considerably, with some utilities available to users only during evening hours. It is best to carefully investigate all aspects of an information utility or network service before making a financial commitment. Over the next several years, we should see a number of network services tailored specifically to the needs of school programs.

Supplementary Writing Software

Other writing tools needed for computer writing programs are spelling checkers, thesauruses, text analysis programs, and integrated writing programs. Spelling checkers may accompany word processing programs or be sold as supplements. Their purpose is to target a misspelled word in the text and display a list of words to replace the misspelled word. Writers then select the correct spelling if it appears, choose to correct the spelling independently if the correct spelling in not among the choices, or leave the word as spelled. Spelling checkers unfortunately cannot evaluate the meanings of words and, as a result, often overlook some misspellings or inappropriate word usage.

Programs that present the suspected misspelling in the context of its sentence or line are preferable to those that present the word either in isolation or as part of a list of possible misspellings at the end of a document. This option enables writers to judge the word in context and also determine its appropriateness. Because many programs have limited dictionaries, an invaluable option for a spelling checker is the capability to add proper names and other frequently misspelled words to the main dictionary. Thesauruses provide a dictionary of synonyms and antonyms that can be used to replace words that are overused in text or may deviate slightly from the writer's intention. The size of the dictionary and the ease of access and use are primary considerations when evaluating both spelling checkers and thesauruses. The instructor also must check that interface is possible between the selected program and the word processing software used in the writing program.

When judging the appropriateness and effectiveness of text analysis programs, the writing instructor should follow guidelines similar to those used to evaluate word processing programs. Ease of use is perhaps the most important consideration. For example, it is essential to know the audience for whom the program was written and then determine the type and amount of instruction necessary to teach students to use the program. Identifying the foci of the program also is necessary. Some programs focus only on word level analysis and neglect sentence level analysis. More comprehensive text analyzers cover several aspects of the writing process and include grammar analysis and mechanical error checks. The number of features that can be analyzed by the program should be identified clearly.

Prompting programs, another type of writing support program, typically provide students with cues and prompts to facilitate planning or revision processes. The most important points to remember when evaluating supplementary programs are how well the analysis or prompting programs relate to the instructional goals of the writing program, how effective is their interface with the word processing program students are using, and how easily students can alternate between word processing and the writing supports.

Figure 7.2.

Comparison of word processors for elementary grades

Word Processing Programs	Price	Miscellaneous Features								Support Features				Writing Tools				Ratings				
		Operation	Mouse	Icons	Column Choice	Typestyles	Frozen Prompts	Merge Files	"Text only" files	Macros	Help Screens	Tutorial	Teacher's Guide	Student Activities	Spelling Checker	Grammar Checker	Thesaurus	Features	Support Features	Ease of Learning	Ease of Use	Value	Overall Score

KEY: Y — YES   N — NO   M — MENU DRIVEN   C — COMMAND DRIVEN
B — BOTH   P — PRINTER   S — SCREEN
RATINGS INDEX: 5 — OUTSTANDING   4 — GOOD   3 — SATISFACTORY
2 — POOR   1 — UNACCEPTABLE
Source: "Mightier than the Typewriter: Using the Computer to Teach Writing
for the Mass Media. A Report on a Conference" (1st, Syracuse, New
York, December 2–4, 1986) Reprinted with permission.

Integrated software programs for writing generally include a
core word processing program and several supplementary
programs that operate in unison or independently. Integrated
software programs can be very useful within a computer-
assisted writing environment because they offer a number of
options, which otherwise would need to be purchased separately as components of a system. Evaluation of integrated
software is based on the effectiveness of the individual
components as well as on their ability to work as an integrated,
efficient writing system.

Conclusion

It seems appropriate to reiterate several aspects of the
evaluation of software and writing tools for computer-assisted

composing. First, instructors should consider the ages and developmental levels of their students and evaluate their writing ability to determine program goals and instructional objectives. Then, both hardware and software for the writing program should be evaluated in light of the characteristics of the students who will use them. Specific guidelines have been developed to use in this evaluation process. In addition to the NCTE guidelines presented earlier, Figures 7.2 and 7.3 exemplify instruments developed specifically to assess the attributes of writing software. Finally, word processing programs and other writing tools should be selected with the intention of continuing the evaluation of their effectiveness for student writers. Software programs should be updated frequently and adapted as the need arises.

Figure 7.3.

EVALUATION FORM FOR WORD PROCESSING PROGRAMS

This form is intended to help you in the important process of evaluating word processing programs for student use. Answer the questions in each section as you examine the program. Use the completed form to aid you in your overall evaluation of the program.

I. GENERAL INFORMATION

1. Program name _____

2. Publisher _____

3. Advertised use (i.e. business, education, etc.) _____

4. Price per unit (special deal for multiple purchases?) _____

5. Available on (machine brand) _____

6. Hardware/Memory Requirements:
   Memory _____ Diskette/Cassette (circle one)

7. Other special hardware requirements? _____

8. Does publisher allow previewing? _____

9. Are back-up disks available, or can they be made? _____

10. Age level of intended user _____

II. MAJOR FUNCTIONS — mark each question Y for Yes or N for No. Add up Yes responses upon completion of each section and fill in as indicated.

1. Documentation
Answers marked yes _____ (out of 7)
Yes/No

_____ 1. Is the documentation well-written?

_____ 2. Is the information concise and direct?

_____ 3. Is the documentation indexed for easy accessibility?

_____ 4. Can students find informaton they need quickly?

_____ 5. Does a summary/reference card come with the manual?

_____ 6. Is the summary card easy to follow and use?

_____ 7. Can the material be duplicated for student use?

2. Directions for Use
Answers marked yes _____ (out of 8)
Yes/No

_____ 1. Is the program screen-directed, that is, can a student tell what to do by looking at the screen?

_____ 2. Can the student use the program without continually looking back at the directions?

_____ 3. Does a tutorial accompany the diskette/cassette?

_____ 4. If so, does the tutorial address most of the major functions?

_____ 5. Is the tutorial easy to use?

_____ 6. Is there a HELP or AID key available for directions?

_____ 7. Does screen question user before major tasks, like *delete paragraph*, and *Quit* (i.e. "Did you save your program?" "Do you want to delete this?")

_____ 8. Can students use print, as well as editor program?

3. Command Simplicity
Answers marked yes _____ (out of 4)
Yes/No

_____ 1. Are commands logical (as in CTRL D for Delete)?

_____ 2. Are most commands single-key commands?

_____ 3. Are commands easily remembered?

_____ 4. If commands are multi-key, are they relatively easy for students to make?

4. Visual Presentation
Answers marked yes _____ (out of 6)
Yes/No

_____ 1. Is print display both upper and lower case?

_____ 2. Do screen margins help focus learner attention and increase readability?

_____ 3. Is there some space between each line of print on the screen?

_____ 4. Is the line length at least 40 characters?

_____ 5. Is the letter shape standard?

_____ 6. Does the program separate lines *between* words, as opposed to splitting words to fit the line length?

5. Audience
Answers marked yes _____ (out of 3)
Yes/No

_____ 1. Is the program appropriate for the students with whom it will be used?

_____ 2. Is the program flexible enough to allow for extended use or use with a wide age/ability range?

_____ 3. Can students successfully use, write, edit, save and print functions?

At this point it might help you to write out a brief summary of your overall impressions of this program. Be sure to mention specific features not covered in this form, or features that you specifically liked or disliked. These will help you make your final decision concerning purchase or use.

MAJOR STRENGTHS OF THE PROGRAM _____

_____

MAJOR WEAKNESSES OF THE PROGRAM _____

_____

GENERAL COMMENTS _____

_____

OVERALL RATING: _____ Excellent _____ Good
_____ Fair _____ Fair

RATER'S NAME _____

DATE OF EVALUATION _____

Source Karen Piper-McGraw, Separating Wheat from Chaff: Evaluating Word Processing Programs for Language Arts instruction. *Computers, Reading and Language Arts, 1* (3), pp. 9–14. Reprinted with permission.

CHAPTER 8

Current Trends and Future Directions

The field of educational computing is characterized by rapid and multidimensional change, leaving educators constantly challenged by new developments that affect classroom learning and teaching. Technology will continue to transform the structure and content of learning across disciplines. By virtue of their profession, educators must keep abreast of trends and issues in the field of educational computing and continually adjust their perspectives by reexamining the benefits, limitations, and implications of technology for education as the future becomes the present. The enormous impact that technology will have on education as we enter the twenty-first century demands that educators refine their thinking about the link between teaching and technology and restructure the educational environment to accommodate new developments in the field. A multitude of barriers must be overcome and problems resolved if educators are to meet these challenges. Collaboration must take place at all levels of the educational community, if computers and other technological aids to learning are to become integral to the educational process. This chapter examines several current trends and future directions in the broad field of educational computing with particular attention given to the effect computers have on writing and language arts instruction.

Trends in Educational Computing

It is estimated that by 1993 there will be over 7 million computers in the elementary and secondary schools for approximately 44 million students, a ratio of approximately one computer to every six students, which translates to about an hour of computer use per day per pupil (Cartwright, 1988). State commissioners of education and other key educational policy makers, in their forecast of learning needs for the remainder of the twentieth century, identified the ability to understand electronic communications, including basic computer operations and word processing (Carrithers, 1987). Do educators have the necessary background and training to provide state-of-the-art technology-based instruction?

In 1988 approximately 60 percent of the incoming freshmen at Pennsylvania State University had some computer competency (Cartwright, 1988). In a few years it will be safe to assume that most students will have had some exposure to computers. Does this mean that students are "computer literate" and well prepared to actively participate in technological learning? They may have some prerequisite skills for computer-based learning but certainly will need well-equipped, well-designed programs to develop and extend these skills. At this point, most schools do not provide an effective computer-based learning environment for students. Bork (1987) estimated that less than 1 percent of learning in the nation's schools in the early 1980s involved computers.

The obvious message from these data is that the technological age is upon us and must be taken seriously by every person in the educational community. According to Bork (1987), computers are destined to become the dominant delivery system at all levels of education and will be the most cost-efficient approach to learning yet. An interesting trend that supports this notion and also relates to the costs of computer-based education is the reduction in the price of hardware. Computers, which have been decreasing in cost by 25 percent per year for equivalent computer power, will continue for a long period of time to become cheaper, smaller, and more powerful (Bork, 1987). Along with advancements in hardware capability is the need to develop high-quality software to complement the increased capabilities of the computer. As

Bork so aptly warned, progress in education will not be achieved simply with large numbers of powerful computers that are not also matched by high-quality computer instructional material.

Gregory Jackson and Judah Schwartz of Harvard University's Center for Research in Educational Computing in their discussion of the future of educational computing identified the following four objectives for computer-based instructional programs (Maddux, 1984). First, they see a need to enlarge the knowledge base about the effectiveness of the computer for learning generally and for learning in specific curricular areas. Second, it is critical to understand how technology fits into the teaching-learning process. Third, understanding the impact on the organizational structure as technology is introduced into the schools is vital. Finally, the ability to gauge technology's fulfillment of the promise to augment the intellectual development and learning potential of children is essential. Jackson and Schwartz also were concerned about how an information society dependent on data processing and telecommunications will affect the value systems and the general structure of society. These are very real issues for educators, who are faced with making daily decisions about educational computing in their schools. Telematics and videotext are two developments that will have tremendous impact on classroom learning over the next several decades.

Telematics

Telecommunications and networks have been called the *source of the turning point* in data processing (Nora and Minc, 1980). Telematics, the merger of computers and telecommunications, is a futuristic conceptualization of information exchange that already has been realized to some extent. Near the turn of the century, telematics is expected to culminate in universal satellites that transmit data with ease and speed. These extremely powerful satellites will be capable of transmitting voice, data, images, sound, and messages, and will become the dominant method of communication. As telematics becomes institutionalized, education's notion of basic skills instruction will expand to include instruction in the concept and practical application of telematics. As we enter the twenty-first century, educators will begin to recognize the importance of preparing youngsters to cope with emerging technology. The environment for learning will simulate and reflect the world as a community where distance no longer is a barrier to communication. Accessibility to networks for communicating with others at local, national, and even international levels is an important aspect of an educational computing environment. Without necessary computer skills and written language skills to participate in a society structured around telematics and information exchange, individuals will be at a distinct economic and social disadvantage. Paisley and Chen (1982) contended that the new technologies depend more on literacy than traditional print media and are intrinsically more motivating for young children as they begin to read and write.

Videotext

Videotext, William Wresch's (1984b) term for electronic or computer-based text, will be the basis for language arts instruction in the future. We are beginning to see the positive effects of an instructional approach where young children learn to read and write simultaneously (Graves, 1983). The underlying concepts of this process approach to instruction easily are adapted to computer-based instruction in the language arts. Chapters Four and Five provided a detailed discussion of the merger of writing process instruction and computer-assisted composing. As computers become a primary mode for language arts learning, the conceptualization of written language may change. The nature of computer interactions and the use of computers as the primary means of communication will change the nature of the communication process. "Talky writing," for instance, where "writers talk their text into the computer and receive a printout instantly" (Daiute, 1985b, p. 291), will become more common than reflective writing. This type of writing is characterized by typical speech patterns that contain incomplete ideas, spelling and grammatical errors, and loosely connected text. This author believes that although writing may decline in quality, the composing process will be simplified for the majority of people, and writing may actually become the preferred method of communication.

Nora and Minc (1980) also argued that "processed language" may endanger the tradition of writing. Preserving and making available standard writing forms to the general population while also promoting coded and abbreviated forms of writing is another challenge facing the educational community. In response to these concerns, Pea and Kurland (1987) imagined "Flexible systems that would allow writers of any skill level, while creating, evaluating, and revising text structures, to tap external stores of knowledge that would radically extend memory—that would, in effect, break down the barriers between mind and machine and facilitate the ready flow of knowledge in the service of writing in an integrated human-computer writing system" (p. 279). In other words, quality of writing would not necessarily be compromised by the advent of the videotext generation. "Talky writing" or "processed language" may simply represent choices on a continuum of writing styles available to individuals.

In her vision of the future, Solomon (1986) sees children using computers as an expressive medium that provides choice at all levels. Learning alternatives will include interactive writing or knowledge-based programs. Choices for communication include speech, typewriter, touch, or body movement. In the future, children will be more flexible as they adapt to different modes of reading and writing. As children become as comfortable with videotext as they are with print, education must modify its current instructional practice. To meet the challenge of videotext and accompanying adaptations, teacher preparation programs must provide prospective teachers with the necessary background and skills to teach communication skills through technology.

Future Hardware

Lower costs of computers in combination with increased capability set the stage for testing the limits of the human-machine partnership. New augmentative devices become available almost daily. Computer magazines and journals usually devote a section to the description of new products. Several examples of state-of-the-art hardware were reported in just one issue of *Electronic Learning* (New Products, 1988). The first, a new workstation called the *Domain Series 10000,* by Apollo Computers, is fast, small, and powerful. This computer promises reduced instruction set computing and increased speed of numerical computations. It has the capability to use four processors in a single workstation. Another product, the Sun-4/110 workstation by SunMicrosystems, delivers seven VAX MIPS for computer-intensive applications and features eight Mb of main memory, a monochrome monitor, 1.3 gigabytes of formatted storage capacity, a low profile keyboard, and an optical mouse pointing device. A third example, a new printer, the LaserPro GoldExpress from OAS Incorporated, prints eight pages per minute and features 1.5 Mb of RAM, the Express Comand Language, 31 standard fonts, 39 built-in barcodes, the Pyramid font generation system, and vector graphics capability. These products, by the way, already have been "upstaged" as this book goes to press. They represent just a few of the choices available to computer consumers. Their descriptions also illustrate a new clipped, coded language or "computerese." It is not difficult to rationalize the need for a staff computer technician who not only has a knowledge of computers, but also keeps abreast of new developments and is able to troubleshoot and repair problems.

Bork (1987) identified several advances to be expected over the next few years. Voice output, for instance, will continue to be refined to more closely approximate human intonation and pitch. Different forms of input, such as painting, voice, brain wave input, and handwriting will become commonplace. Music and graphics, both of which have considerable motivational value for computer users, will become options on many programs. Improved graphics will bring more choice in color, resolution, shading, intensity control, and animation. Text production will be expanded, with greater choice among fonts and size of text. More publication and multimedia production opportunities will arise as systems become more compatible. As a final note, even with these highly sophisticated components, computers will become more, rather than less, user friendly.

Future Software

Advances in software have not always kept pace with comparable advances in hardware. The industry is just beginning to produce knowledge-based programs that can seriously compete with traditional presentation of material. Although much software has been produced, its quality and effectiveness have been questioned by computer experts (Bork, 1987). Within the past few years, however, software producers have begun to make a transition from low-level, poor-quality programs to more sophisticated programs. This is nowhere more evident than in the area of writing tools. Many of these rely on some type of expert system. Expert systems are highly sophisticated branching programs that replicate human information processing and provide the foundation for complex, interactive instructional models. Multiple path models are replacing linear models for software design. Integrated software that combines tutoring, coaching, simulation, and drill and practice should enhance learning and instruction by creating more choices for learners and teachers and by being more personalized in their approach.

In their description of the movement toward computer-based writing tools and computer-based writing instruction, Pea and Kurland (1987) identified four primary phases:

1. Typewriter technology.

2. Mainframe writing tools.

3. Microcomputer writing tools.

4. The most recent embarkation, cognitive technologies.

Whereas phase 3 is characterized by direct writing supports such as text planning programs and prewriting tools, phase 4 represents a futuristic leap into computer technology that provides direct support by emulating the thought processes of writers. This phase, facilitated by developments in artificial intelligence and "natural-language understanding," will provide more intelligent feedback from computers about the structure and semantics of writing.

As part of this revolution in cognitive technology, Sharples envisioned a package of software to help children acquire, store, and manipulate knowledge as they explore different media for communicating through language, sound, and pictures. In his view, integrated systems must be able to solve problems, model solutions, tolerate errors, and provide feedback in language easily understood by children. Writers will be able to program the system in simple, descriptive language to accommodate and satisfy the various constraints associated with the writing process such as style, structure, and format, thus freeing them to experiment with "the world of thought and language" (Sharples, 1985, p. 110). Several integrated systems that begin to approximate the model suggested by Sharples are described in the Appendix.

Videodisk technology is yet another innovation that will have a tremendous impact on instruction in all areas. It is possible that with reduced costs over the next few years intelligent videodisk materials will become more accessible to schools than they are currently. The high-quality computer-video interactive materials thus far produced have been too expensive for most schools to adopt. This is unfortunate, because these programs by nature are highly interactive and have many more capabilities than programs without a video component.

Production of intelligent videodisk learning materials can be approached from several directions (Bork, 1987). It is possible to start with educational film material and simply add interactive computer capabilities. A second approach is to start with excellent, field-tested software and develop slides, video sequences, and sound to increase the learning effectiveness of the material. Third, material already available in videodisk form can be added to the computer. The fourth approach is the most expensive, in that an entire package of slides, video, audio, and computer-based materials is developed by a design team. Team members bring their different backgrounds and areas of expertise for a multidisciplinary approach to software development.

Interactive videodisk materials for writing instruction are particularly intriguing. In essence, these videodisk programs would incorporate features of integrated computer writing software with effective instructional video sequences. Students would learn the writing process through interactive participation.

Young (1984) believed that videodisk simulations are as or more effective than traditional formats for instruction and assessment. Studies have identified several positive aspects of learning through videodisk simulations (Soled et al., 1989; Young, 1984). The support for the use of videodisk simulations in instructional programs stems from evidence of reduced learning time and simplified evaluation techniques. Built-in criterion-referenced evaluations provide the opportunity to evaluate and monitor progress of students functioning at varying levels of ability and understanding. Intelligent videodisk instruction currently is the most exciting, if not the most sophisticated, technological approach to education.

Computer Environment for Writing and Learning

Several interesting ideas about the electronic learning environment of the future have been proposed. Gibbon (1983) asserted that the electronic environment for learning will extend beyond the school to the home, workplace, library, and commercially operated computer and information centers. He conceptualized electronic learning devices to include broadcast television, satellite television, one-way and two-way cable television, teletext, viewdata, teleconferencing, videodisks, video cassettes, home computers, computers linked in networks, computers with a range of input and output mechanisms, communication linkage systems, databanks, and specialized information banks. These devices will be available to and essentially controlled by the learner. Gibbon (1983) identified several characteristics of the electronic learning environments as particularly important to their success.

First, Gibbon saw the need for an environment that is flexible and responsive to individual learners. At the same time, teaching students how to take control of their learning and the learning environment is important. The electronic system should be capable of presenting both images and alphanumeric information. The environment should be structured around a communication network and characterized by multimodal interactions and dynamic learning experiences that reflect reality. Finally, the environment should have in place a communication network. This last feature is particularly relevant to the computer writing environment. The communication capabilities of computers already far exceed the expectations of only a few years ago.

Interestingly, we are just beginning to see the influence of this powerful capability on composition classes. As technology becomes less expensive, computer networks will become a standard feature of the learning environment. Experimentation with networking and writing instruction so far has been limited to a few studies with elementary and secondary learners (Levin et al., 1985). Because of the access to mainframe computers and minicomputers on university campuses, most of the networked writing classes currently are found at the community college and university level.

The fusion of telecommunications and computers creates infinite possibilities for education. As a result of extensive use of computer networks in classrooms, major changes will occur in the social and temporal structure of the educational process. The roles of teachers and administrators will be altered by these changes. As a final note, it seems necessary to address the need for universities to prepare educators to meet the challenges of technology-based education.

Professional Preparation Programs

A new model of teaching and learning is on the horizon. In this mode, students, teachers, and computers make up an interactive learning unit characterized by cooperation and collaboration. As this new form of instruction replaces traditional models of instruction, universities must assume responsibility for adequately preparing teachers to function effectively within this new "collaborative system." Teachers must be prepared for their new roles as facilitator and guide and must be better prepared to enhance the cognitive development of children within an educational computing environment. This new environment will emphasize thinking and reasoning rather than acquisition of facts. Student progress will be measured very differently as the emphasis shifts to process assessment and cognitive learning models. Computers will be directly involved in measuring student progress as well as managing instruction.

For these changes to occur smoothly, universities must lead the way by changing the nature of instruction. Not only is it necessary that universities complement the emerging technology-based instructional programs in secondary and elementary schools by providing state-of-the-art teacher preparation programs, but also that they provide a model for classroom instruction. Computer-based college composition classes already have begun to incorporate sophisticated networked writing programs that support collaborative and cooperative learning. These models of the learning environment provide teachers-in-training with actual computer-based learning experiences that will be replicated in their classrooms.

Hawkins and Sheingold (1986) predicted that an ungraded computer learning environment will permit students to learn at their own developmental pace as they acquire skills for independent learning. Emphasis will be placed on teaching students to find, synthesize, and interpret information. Schools will be forums for discussion and information exchange rather than the source of information. "Textbooks" will be updated automatically, so information always is current and accurate.

Bork (1987) fears that the shortage of math, science, and computer science instructors at all educational levels will retard the development of high-quality educational computing programs. He suggests that computer-based curriculum development be carefully organized, adequately financed, and involve the best faculty members and specialists from different universities and private corporations. Universities should recognize and encourage faculty members in this endeavor. Research to study computer-based learning must be supported through university programs in cooperation with the government, major corporations, and private foundations if we are to establish an effective computer learning environment in our nation's schools.

Conclusion

As Alvin Toffler wrote in 1974, "all education springs from some image of the future" (p. 3). The future of education depends on embracing computers as a crucial link in the educational process. It resides in accepting the limitless opportunities that technology affords students as they learn to take responsibility and become independent thinkers in a society that frequently seems to undermine that possibility. Computer-based education has the potential to expand the learning experiences of children by providing alternatives and choices that will enable them to be literate, informed, and successful in their own right.

APPENDIX
COMPUTER-ASSISTED COMPOSING SOFTWARE

Word Processors

Bank Street Writer

Appropriate for all ages.

Easy to learn and use menu-driven programs. Has text movement, search and replace, and automatic centering. Includes tutorial and utility programs, a reference manual, and a back-up disk.

Computing-Operating
    System: Apple II + /IIe and Commodore
                              64 (64K), IBM PC/PCjr and Apple
                              IIe/IIc (128K)

Distributor: Scholastic Publications
                              730 Broadway
                              New York, NY 10003

Betterworking Wordprocessor

Appropriate for age 12–adult.

Drop-down menus and "what you see is what you get" printing. Includes an outliner, 100,000 word spelling checker, and a full range of text editing, layout, and formatting functions.

Computing-Operating
    System: IBM PC

Distributor: Spinnaker Software
                                 One Kendall Square
                                 Cambridge, MA 02139

Cotton Tales

Appropriate for grades 1–3.

Designed for young children, the program combines simple word processing, picture menus, large-type words, and built-in editor.

Computing-Operating
    System: Apple II, 48K

Distributor: Opportunities for Learning, Inc.
                                 20417 Nordhoff St.
                                 Dept. A4S
                                 Chatsworth, CA 91311

Elf Word Processor

Appropriate for grades 1–9.

Teaches young children the basics and essential features of word processing including insert, delete, save, load, and print.

Computing-Operating
    System: Apple II, 48K

Distributor: Opportunities for Learning, Inc.
                                 20417 Nordhoff St.
                                 Dept. A4S
                                 Chatsworth, CA 91311

FrEdWriter

Appropriate for grades 2–12.

Based on a public domain program, this word processing program has built-in prompted writing capabilities to guide students through the writing process. Intended to be freely duplicated and used with students.

Computing-Operating
   System: Apple family

Distributor: CUE SoftSwap
                       P.O. Box 271704
                       Concord, CA 94527-1704

Grolier Writer

Appropriate for grades 3–9.

Designed for students with no word processing experience, the menu-driven program has a graphic, on-screen tutorial and a range of editing functions.

Computing-Operating
   System: Apple II, 64K

Distributor: Opportunities for Learning, Inc.
                       20417 Nordhoff St.
                       Dept. A4S
                       Chatsworth, CA 91311

Homeword

Appropriate for grades 1–12.

Program uses icons, or picture symbols, to represent program functions and guide students through the editing process. Includes a tutorial audio cassette, comprehensive instruction book, and built-in spelling checker with over 28,000 words.

Computing-Operating
   System: Apple 64K and 128K/ProDOS

Distributor: Opportunities for Learning, Inc.
                       20417 Nordhoff St.
                       Dept. A4S
                       Chatsworth, CA 91311

II Write

Appropriate for grades 4 and up.

Program features pull-down menus; a variety of fonts, type styles, and sizes; a screen display that matches the printed document; and multiple windows for editing up to four documents at the same time. Works with keyboard or mouse. Includes user's guide, teacher's resource manual, and student activities disk.

Computing-Operating
    System: Apple II (2 disk drives), 128K

Distributor: Opportunities for Learning, Inc.
                                   20417 Nordhoff St.
                                   Dept. A4S
                                   Chatsworth, CA 91311

Kidwriter

Appropriate for grades pre-K–3.

Stories are written to accompany picture settings created by selecting from a variety of "picture pieces." Fundamentals of word and image processing are introduced.

Computing-Operating
    System: Apple II family, Commodore, IBM PC

Distributor: Learning Well
                                   Dept. D
                                   299 South Service Road
                                   Roslyn Heights, NY 11577

Magic Slate II

Appropriate for grades 2–adult.

Features special typestyles; 20-, 40-, and 80-column levels; cut and paste capabilities; picture menu and simplified commands for beginners; and a Student Planner for invisible prewriting. Special teacher options create custom files and lessons.

Computing-Operating
    System: Apple II family, 128K, graphic
                                   printer desired

Distributor: Sunburst Communications
                                   39 Washington Avenue
                                   Pleasantville, NY 10570-2898

Mastertype's Writer

Appropriate for grades 2–12.

Word processor with window feature, built-in tutorial, dial windows, database, and simple correction commands. Multiple type faces and color highlighting.

Computing-Operating
System: Apple II family, Commodore 64

Distributor: Learning Well
                          Dept. D
                          299 South Service Road
                          Roslyn Heights, NY 11577

MECC Writer

Appropriate for age 6–adult.

Writers learn one initial word processing system, described by the publisher as efficient and easy to use. Can be adapted to other MECC packages and systems.

Computing-Operating
System: Apple 64K GS

Publisher: MECC
                          3490 Lexington Avenue North
                          St. Paul, Minnesota 55126

Mousewrite

Appropriate for grades 3–12.

The printer capabilities include underlining, bold, wide margins, subscripts, superscripts, and italics. Other features include multiple windows, clipboard, and spelling checker. Can be used with a mouse.

Computing-Operating
System: Apple IIc or enhanced IIe with
                          extended 80-column card

Distributor: Opportunities for Learning, Inc.
                                     20417 Nordhoff St.
                                     Dept. A4S
                                     Chatsworth, CA 91311

Multiscribe 2.0

Appropriate for age 10–adult.

A variety of fonts, type styles, character sizes, and text formatting options are available with this word processing package. A spelling checker and additional Fontpak are available.

Computing-Operating
    System: Apple IIe/IIc/IIGS, 128K

Distributor: Opportunities for Learning, Inc.
                                     20417 Nordhoff St.
                                     Dept. A4S
                                     Chatsworth, CA 91311

Multiscribe GS

Appropriate for age 10–adult.

In addition to the features of Multiscribe 2.0, this program offers multiple windows to work on several documents simultaneously.

Computing-Operating
    System: Apple IIGS, 512K

Distributor: Opportunities for Learning, Inc.
                                     20417 Nordhoff St.
                                     Dept. A4S
                                     Chatsworth, CA 91311

Muppet Slate

Appropriate for grades K–2.

To be used with Muppet Learning Keys, this word and picture processor enables students to use an alphabet picture book and use Rebus writing to create stories.

Computing-Operating
    System: Apple IIe, IIc, IIGS, 64K

Distributor: Sunburst Communications
                                    39 Washington Avenue
                                    Pleasantville, NY 19570-2898

Sensible Writer

Appropriate for age 12–adult.

Used for effective professional documents and has ability to handle two large documents simultaneously. It has additional grammar and spelling programs.

Computing-Operating
    System: Apple II + /IIc/IIGS, or an
                                    enhanced IIe,128K

Distributor: Opportunities for Learning, Inc.
                                    20417 Nordhoff St.
                                    Dept. A4S
                                    Chatsworth, CA 91311

Text Tiger

Appropriate for grades 2 and up.

Four games, on one side of the disk, are used to introduce students to word processing features and provide practice in writing and editing. Word processing program is on the reverse side of the disk.

Computing-Operating
    System: Apple II, 48K

Distributor: Opportunities for Learning, Inc.
                                    20417 Nordhoff St.
                                    Dept. A4S
                                    Chatsworth, CA 91311

Webster's New World Writer

Appropriate for age 12–adult.

This program prints exactly what is on the screen and has over 500 help screens. Various capabilities include search and replace, recovery keys, and a graphics mode as well as an on-line thesaurus and spelling checker with a database of over 114,000 words. It also has the capability to correct typographical errors, phonetic misspellings, and transpositions.

Computing-Operating
    System: IBM, 256K

Distributor: Opportunities for Learning, Inc.
                        20417 Nordhoff St.
                        Dept. A4S
                        Chatsworth, CA 91311

WordPerfect 5.0

Appropriate for age 12–adult.

An update on previous versions, WordPerfect is a graphically oriented package with a large collection of programs, dictionaries, font definitions, and other support files. Includes improved font management features and a preview feature that magnifies a document 200 percent. Has a Setup menu, mnemonic devices for remembering commands, and three predefined key layouts. Other features include the ability to edit more than one document at a time; excellent mail merge and sorting options; extensive on-line help, and automatic indexing, table of contents, referencing, and footnoting.

Computing-Operating
    System: IBM, 640K

Distributor: WordPerfect Corporation
                        1555 North Technology Way
                        Orem, UT 84057

Wordstar Easy

Appropriate for age 6–adult.

Includes single key commands, easy-to-read menus and screens, easy access to multiple type styles, on-screen boldface and underlining, and built-in spelling corrector.

Computing-Operating
    System: IBM PC, 64K

Distributor: Opportunities for Learning, Inc.
20417 Nordhoff St.
Dept. A4S
Chatsworth, CA 91311

Wordstar

Appropriate for age 10–adult.

Students progress from simple on-screen commands to sophisticated word processing features including a mail merge option.

Computing-Operating
    System: Apple II and IBM PC, 64K

Distributor: Opportunities for Learning, Inc.
20417 Nordhoff St.
Dept. A4S
Chatsworth, CA 91311

The Write Choice

Appropriate for age 7–adult.

Easy to learn with simple, on-screen formatting. Offers most word processing features including displayed page breaks, cut and paste, find and replace, underlining, and bold print. Package includes a typing tutorial, a readability analyst, and a style manual.

Computing-Operating
    System: Apple II, II+, IIe, or IIGS

Distributor: Roger Wagner Publishing, Inc.
1050 Pioneer Way, Suite "P"
El Cajon, CA 92020

Writer's Choice Elite

Appropriate for grade 4 and up.

Specifically designed for the Apple IIGS, this word processor writes and highlights in color as writers view up to sixteen documents simultaneously.

Computing-Operating
    System: Apple IIGS, 512K

Distributor: Opportunities for Learning, Inc.
                              20417 Nordhoff St.
                              Dept. A4S
                              Chatsworth, CA 91311

Word Processing with Speech Synthesis

Dr. Peet's Talk/Writer

Appropriate for grades pre-K–3.

A two-disk package, this user-friendly system helps students learn to recognize and say their ABC's as well as develop keyboard and on-line word processing skills. A "talking" word processor is used in conjunction with the Echo speech synthesizer (Cricket synthesizer for IIc), which reads the text as it is written. The program features talk/no talk options, large type, print capability, phonetic adjustments for words with difficult or quirky pronunciations, an individual filing system, and special typing options for blind students. The text can be printed in large letters on the Apple Imagewriter, Epson, or Apple Dot Matrix printers.

Computing-Operating
    System: Apple II +, IIc, and IIe

Publisher: Hartley Courseware, Inc.
                              Box 419
                              Dimondale, MI 48821

Keytalk

Appropriate for ages 3–8.

Based on the language experience approach to teaching written language, this software uses one disk and six sample commands for producing text, has speech output capabilities to read what is written, has a feature to correct speech output errors, and includes the capacity to develop a dictionary on the disk. For very young children, the authors recommend using the Muppet Learning Keys keyboard, published by Sunburst Communications, and the Echo or Cricket speech synthesizer.

Computing-Operating
    System: Apple II +, IIc, and IIe.

Publisher: Peal Software, Inc.
                                  3200 Wilshire Blvd.
                                  Suite 1207 South Tower
                                  Los Angeles, CA 90010

My Words

Appropriate for grades K–3.

In addition to the capabilities of *Dr. Peet's Talk/Writer,* this talking word processor includes a built-in electronic word box that automatically adds and alphabetizes each new word the child types. Students can use a mouse, joystick, touch window, or keyboard to select words for automatic inclusion in their writing. They can hear their words pronounced and can print their text and word bank. The Echo speech synthesizer is required.

Computing-Operating
    System: Apple IIe, IIc, or IIGS

Publisher: Hartley Courseware, Inc.
                                  Box 419
                                  Dimondale, MI 48821

Talking Text Writer

Appropriate for grades K–9.

This is a fully functioning word processor, developed primarily for special needs children. One disk was created for reading and writing; another for reading only. The program includes a dictionary feature for creating, storing, and recalling a definition for any word on the text screen. Students can select 20-, 40-, or 80-column text. Uses the Echo + voice synthesizer (Cricket synthesizer for the Apple IIc).

Computing-Operating
    System: Apple IIe, IIc, IIGS; Franklin ACE 2000

Publisher: Scholastic Software
                            730 Broadway
                            New York, NY 10003

Keyboard Tutorials

Betterworking Typing Made Easy

Appropriate for age 12–adult.

Drill-based programmed keyboard instruction with progress analysis and individualized progress reports.

Computing-Operating
    System: IBM PC, Apple IIe, IIc, II + /64K

Distributor: Spinnaker Software
                            One Kendall Square
                            Cambridge, MA 02139

FrEdTyper

Appropriate for grades 4–12.

Consists of forty prompted file lessons for practicing touch typing skills. Accuracy can be checked either on-screen or in printout.

Computing-Operating
    System: Apple family

Distributor: CUE SoftSwap
                            P.O. Box 271704
                            Concord, CA 94527-1704

Keyboard Cadet

Appropriate for grades 2–12.

On-screen graphics show a keyboard and correct fingering. Game format including word, sentence, and timed paragraph typing with progress records for 100 students.

Computing-Operating
     System: Apple II family, IBM PC, IBM
                                 PCjr, Tandy 1000

Distributor: Mindscape, Inc.
                                 Educational Division
                                 Dept. D
                                 344 Dundee Road
                                 Northbrook, IL 60062

Muppet Learning Keys

Appropriate for grades pre-K–1.

Designed for young children. Features include upper- and
lower-case letters in sequential order on the keyboard, keys to
activate the use of upper- and lower-case letters, and "action"
buttons (Stop, Go, Erase, and Print). May be used with a
joystick port.

Computing-Operating
     System: Apple IIe, IIc, IIGS, 64K

Distributor: Sunburst Communications
                                 39 Washington Avenue
                                 Pleasantville, NY 10570-2898

Type to Learn

Appropriate for grades 2–adult.

A complete keyboarding course using a language-based format.
Special features include primary and advanced vocabulary
levels, individualized speed and accuracy goals, game menu,
animated "hands" to teach and correct errors, and automatic
record-keeping for progress reports.

Computing-Operating
     System: Apple II, 64K; IBM, 128K or
                                 256K; Tandy 1000, 256K

Distributor: Sunburst Communications
                                 39 Washington Avenue
                                 Pleasantville, NY 10570-2898

Tut's Typer

Appropriate for age 8–adult.

Teaches touch-typing by displaying a dynamic, interactive graphic keyboard on-screen that shows proper finger placement as the student types. Includes teacher-designed lesson capability, preplanned lessons, and teacher utilities to monitor and record progress.

Computing-Operating
    System: Apple IIe, IIGS, IIGS-Dvorak

Distributor: Roger Wagner Publishing, Inc.
                        1050 Pioneer Way, Suite "P"
                        El Cajon, CA 92020

Type to Learn

Appropriate for grades 2–adult.

A language-based program that teaches keyboarding skills while reinforcing spelling, grammar, composition, and punctuation. Includes two vocabulary levels and an option to individualize speed and accuracy goals for up to thirty students. Animated hands teach and help correct errors as they occur.

Computing-Operating
    System: Apple II family, 64K

Distributor: Sunburst Communications
                        39 Washington Avenue
                        Pleasantville, NY 10570-2898

Typing Well

Appropriate for grades 3–adult.

Uses five games to teach touch-typing skills. Word-per-minute speeds can be adjusted for each player.

Computing-Operating
    System: Apple II family

Distributor: Learning Well
                        Dept. D
                        200 South Service Road
                        Roslyn Heights, NY 11577

Genre-Based Programs

Author! Author!

Appropriate for grades 2–12.

A playwright's toolkit complete with backdrops, props, character graphics, and word processing features. The writer enters dialogue and then sees the play acted out on-screen or printed out with graphics. Built-in outlines or playbill options.

Computing-Operating
    System: Apple II family

Distributor: Learning Well
                             Dept. D
                             200 South Service Road
                             Roslyn Heights, NY 11577

CAW: Computer Assisted Writing

Appropriate for grades 7–12.

Includes a built-in word processor and guides students through the processes for developing a business letter of complaint, a report using computer-generated notes, and a persuasive composition.

Computing-Operating
    System: IBM PC

Distributor: Educational Activities, Inc.
                             P.O. Box 392
                             Freeport, NY 11520

Create with Garfield

Appropriate for grades pre-K–3.

A two-disk program with over 200 pieces of artwork, a variety of typefaces for writing captions and stories, capability for printing in color, and electronic moving cartoons. Stimulates children to create stories about a cartoon character.

Computing-Operating
    System: Apple II family, Commodore
                             64/128K

Distributor: Developmental Learning
Materials
1 DLM Park
Allen, TX 75002

Be a Writer

Appropriate for grades 3–7.

Consists of twenty-five lessons which use a building-block method to encourage students to write with full sentences using descriptive, narrative, and explanatory writing styles.

Computing-Operating
System: Apple, 48K

Distributor: Sunburst Communications
39 Washington Avenue
Pleasantville, NY 10570-2898

Homework Helper—Writing

Appropriate for ages 12–18.

Assists students in creating ideas, organizing notes, and writing essays and book reports. Built-in prompts and complete word processing program with spelling checker.

Computing-Operating
System: IBM PC/128K; Apple IIe, IIc,
II + /64K

Distributor: Spinnaker Software
One Kendall Square
Cambridge, MA 02139

I Can Write

Appropriate for grades 2–7.

Consists of twenty-five lessons which range from open-ended explorations of personal identity to more formal language objectives.

Computing-Operating
    System: Apple, 48K

Distributor: Sunburst Communications
                             39 Washington Avenue
                             Pleasantville, NY 10570-2898

Poetry Express

Appropriate for grades 2–12.

Pattern reminders guide students line-by-line as they develop poems. Rhyme, limerick, litany, haiku, sijo, diamante, tank, and cinquain styles included in an easy-edit program.

Computing-Operating
    System: Apple II family, Commodore

Distributor: Learning Well
                             Dept. D
                             200 South Service Road
                             Roslyn Heights, NY 11577

Prewrite

Appropriate for grades 4–8 (Level 1) and grades 9–12 (Level 2).

Presents a springboard of interactive questions and answers to help students brainstorm and produce a printout of concepts for developing a first draft for writing assignments. Prewrite data can be transferred to nearly any word processor in the preparation of reports, proposals, and themes. Program can be customized with special insert mode.

Computing-Operating
    System: Apple II +, IIe, IIc

Distributor: Mindscape, Inc.
                             Educational Division
                             Dept. D
                             344 Dundee Road
                             Northbrook, IL 60062

Show Time

Appropriate for grades 6–9.

Designed to assist students in writing, editing, practicing, and performing their own short plays.

Computing-Operating
System: Apple IIGS, 64K

Distributor: MECC
                                 3490 Lexington Avenue North
                                 St. Paul, MN 55126

Snoopy Writer

Appropriate for grades 1–4.

Generates full-color pictures of Peanuts characters along with story starters and guides students through the story writing, editing, and printing process.

Computing-Operating
System: Apple II series, 64K

Distributor: Random House Media
                                 400 Hahn Road
                                 Westminster, MD 21157

Story Builder

Appropriate for grades 2–6.

By mixing and matching story elements, students can create stories. Embedded are lessons on syntax, analysis, and comprehension. Three levels of difficulty and graphics are available.

Computing-Operating
System: Apple II series, 64K; TRS-80
                                 Model III, 4, 48K

Distributor: Random House Media
                                 400 Hahn Road
                                 Westminster, MD 21157

Story Writer

Appropriate for grades 3–8.

Includes word processing program with over forty pictures suggesting fables, adventures, and emotions as story motivators.

Computing-Operating
    System: Apple II family

Distributor: Learning Well
                              Dept. D
                              200 South Service Road
                              Roslyn Heights, NY 11577

Teddy Bear-rels of Fun

Appropriate for grades pre-K–3.

Designed for young children to create Teddy Bear stories using artwork and a variety of typefaces and print in color or monotone.

Computing-Operating
    System: Apple II family, Commodore
                              64/128K

Distributor: Developmental Learning
                              Materials
                              1 DLM Park
                              Allen, TX 75002

That's My Story

Appropriate for grades 2–12.

Contains story starters and "what if" suggestions. Easy-to-learn word processing and room to insert forty student- or teacher-generated story starters.

Computing-Operating
    System: Apple II, IBM

Distributor: Learning Well
                              Dept. D
                              200 South Service Road
                              Roslyn Heights, NY 11577

Write a Story

Appropriate for grades 5–7.

Using a journey into the future as a motivator, students develop the plot, create characters, and write dialogue for a novella.

Computing-Operating
   System: Apple, 48K

Distributor: Sunburst Communications
                              39 Washington Avenue
                              Pleasantville, NY 10570-2898

Write with Me

Appropriate for grades 4–7.

Students develop a story from title page to conclusion. Each of twenty-five lessons consists of a chapter. Develops narrative writing skills.

Computing-Operating
   System: Apple, 48K

Distributor: Sunburst Communications
                              39 Washington Avenue
                              Pleasantville, NY 10570-2898

The Writing Adventure

Appropriate for ages 9 and up.

Using an adventure story format, this package teaches word processing in conjunction with the writing process. Includes word processing capabilities for writing notes and stories, a proofing aid that checks for common writing errors, and an option to print notes and stories up to four-pages long.

Computing-Operating
   System: Apple II family, Commodore
                              64/128K

Distributor: Developmental Learning
                              Materials
                              1 DLM Park
                              Allen, TX 75002

Writing Process Workshop

Appropriate for grades 5–12.

Designed to simultaneously develop writing and word processing skills, this package includes templates for developing the following composition types: persuasive essay, information report, autobiographical incident, evaluation, biographical sketch, eyewitness memoir, and narrative composition. Includes the FrEdWriter word processor.

Computing-Operating
  System: Apple IIe, Apple IIGS

Distributor: Educational Activities, Inc.
                             P.O. Box 392
                             Freeport, NY 11520

Integrated Writing Programs

HBJ Writer (formerly WANDAH)

Appropriate for secondary and college-level composition courses.

A comprehensive program that combines word processing with routines designed to assist students in prewriting (freewriting, nutshelling, planning, invisible writing), writing, editing (word usage, punctuation, spelling), and revising (organization, style, commenting on a paper). Includes a spelling checker with over 40,000 words, step-by-step operating instructions, a disk that prepares blank disks to store papers, a keyboard template to identify special function keys, and a reference card that summarizes essential keyboard commands.

Computing-Operating
  System: IBM PC (256K, two double-sided
                             disk drives)

Distributor: Harcourt Brace Jovanovich
                             Publishers
                             7555 Caldwell Avenue
                             Chicago, IL 60648

Medley

Appropriate for grades 3–12.

An integrated desktop publishing package that includes full-featured word processing, page layout, and graphics.

Operates with a mouse and prints exactly what appears on the screen. Complete page layout capability allows for unlimited customized columns, text wrapping around any shape, and multiple pages.

Computing-Operating
System: Apple IIGS, 1 Meg RAM, 3.5" Disk
                        Drive (Color RGB Monitor and
                        second disk drive are
                        recommended.)

Distributor: Milliken Publishing Company
                        1100 Research Blvd.
                        P.O. Box 21579
                        St. Louis, MO 63132

Multiscribe

Appropriate for grades 4–12.

A desktop publishing package that contains a word processor and total text and graphics package. Pull-down menus operated with or without a mouse. Products sold separately.

Computing-Operating
System: Apple IIe, IIc, 128K

Distributor: Scholastic, Inc.
                        P.O. Box 7502
                        2931 East McCarty Street
                        Jefferson City, MO 65102

Wordbench

Appropriate for grades 7–adult.

Includes a full-featured word processor and an easy-to-learn menu structure with context-sensitive help screens. Other features are an outliner, notetaker, reference tools for recording bibliographic information, 60,000 word speller, 40,000 word thesaurus, and a brainstormer designed to help writers overcome writer's block. Also includes shortcuts (macros) that allow users to tailor the program to individual writing needs.

Computing-Operating
    System: IBM PC, 256K; Apple IIe, IIc, IIGS, 128K

Distributor: Addison-Wesley
                             Reading, MA 01867

Writer's Helper

Appropriate for grades 8–12.

Consists of twenty-two miniprograms designed to teach the writing process by helping students progress from brainstorming to prewriting, from selecting a topic to researching, then to drafting and editing. Can be linked to a word processor.

Computing-Operating
    System: Apple 64K (an 80-column card is required)

Distributor: Scholastic Inc.
                             730 Broadway
                             New York, NY 10003

Speech Synthesizers (Echo +, Echo IIB, and Echo IIC)

Appropriate for all ages

Computing-Operating
    System: DOS or PRODOS

Distributor: Street Electronics
                             1140 Mark Avenue
                             Carpenteria, CA 93013

BIBLIOGRAPHY

Ammon, P. 1985. Helping children learn to write in English as a second language: Some observations and some hypotheses. In *The acquisition of written language: Response and revision,* ed. S. Freedman, 65–84. Norwood, N.J.: Ablex.

Anderson, D. 1982. Microcomputers in education. *Journal of Learning Disabilities* 15: 368–369.

Anderson, J. R. 1983. *The architecture of cognition.* Cambridge, Mass.: Harvard University Press.

Anderson, R.C. 1978. Schema directed processes in language comprehension. In *Cognitive psychology and instruction,* ed. A. Lesgold, J. Pellegrino, S. Fokhema, and R. Glaser, 67–82. New York: Plenum.

Applebee, A. 1981. *Writing in the secondary school: English and the content areas.* Urbana, Ill.: National Council of Teachers of English.

——. 1986. Problems in process approaches: Toward a reconceptualization of process instruction. In *The teaching of writing,* ed. A. Petrosky and D. Bartholomae, 95–113. Chicago: National Society for the Study of Education.

Applebee, A., J. Langer, and I. Mullis. 1986. *The writing report card: Writing achievement in the schools.* Princeton, N.J.: Educational Testing Service.

Barraga, N. 1983. *Visual handicaps and learning.* Austin: Exceptional Resources.

Batey, A., and D. Ricketts. 1987. Word processors and writing activities for the elementary grades: A MicroSIFT quarterly report. ERIC Document Reproduction Service No. ED 281 211.

Beal, C., and E. Griffin. 1987. Learning to use a text editor. ERIC Document Reproduction Service No. ED 287 459.

Beaugrande, R. de. 1984. *Text Production: Toward a science of composition.* Norwood, N.J.: Ablex.

Behrmann, M. 1984. *Handbook of microcomputers in special education.* San Diego, Calif.: College-Hill Press.

Bereiter, C., and M. Scardamalia. 1987. *The psychology of written expression.* Hillsdale, N.J.: Lawrence Erlbaum Associates.

Biggs, J. B., and K. F. Collis. 1982. *Evaluating the quality of learning: The SOLO taxonomy.* New York: Academic Press.

Bigley, A. 1987. An investigation of microcomputer use in three high school writing programs. Doctoral dissertation, Columbia University Teachers College, 1986. *Dissertation Abstracts International* 47: 4066.

Bilingual Education Act. 1984. Public Law 98-511. Ninety-eighth Congress (October).

Bizzell, P. 1986. Composing processes: An overview. In *The teaching of writing,* ed. A. Petrosky and D. Bartholomae,

49–70. Chicago: National Society for the Study of Education.

Bloom, L., and M. Lahey. 1978. *Language development and language disorders.* New York: John Wiley and Sons.

Boone, R. 1986. The revision processes of elementary school students who write using a word processing computer program. Doctoral dissertation, University of Oregon, 1985. *Dissertation Abstracts International* 47: 155A.

Borgh, K., and W. Dickson. 1986. The effects on children's writing of adding speech synthesis to a word processor. Madison: Wisconsin Center for Education Research. ERIC Document Reproduction Service No. ED 277 007.

Bork, A. 1987. *Learning with personal computers.* New York: Harper and Row.

Bos, C. 1988. Process-oriented writing: Instructional implications for mildly handicapped students. *Exceptional Children* 54: 521–527.

Bracewell, R. J. 1983. Investigating the control of writing skills. In *Research on writing: Principles and methods,* ed. P. Mosenthal, L. Tamor, and S. Walmsley, 177–203. New York: Longman.

Brady, M., and P. Dickson. 1983. Microcomputer communication game for hearing-impaired students. *American Annals of the Deaf* 128: 835–841.

Bramer, M. 1984. Intelligent knowledge based systems. In *New information technology,* ed. A. Burns, 148–158. Chichester, England: Ellis Horwood Limited.

Bridwell, L., G. Sirc, and R. Brook. 1985. Revising and computing: Case studies of student writers. In *The*

acquisition of written language: Response and revision,
ed. S. Freedman, 172–194. Norwood, N.J.: Ablex.

Brisk, M. 1985. Using the computer to develop literacy. *Equity and Choice* 1: 25–32.

Broudy, H. S. 1986. Technology and citizenship. In *Microcomputers and education,* ed. J. A. Culbertson and L. L. Cunningham, 234–253. Chicago: National Society for the Study of Education.

Brown, A. L. 1978. Knowing when, where, and how to remember: A problem of metacognition. In *Advances in instructional psychology,* ed. R. Glaser, 77–165. Hillsdale, N.J.: Lawrence Erlbaum Associates.

Bryson, M. 1986. Augmented word-processing: The influence of task characteristics and mode of production on writers' cognitions. Paper presented at the Annual Meeting of the American Educational Research Association, April, San Francisco.

Burnett, J. 1986. Word processing as a writing tool of an elementary school student. Doctoral dissertation, University of Maryland, 1984. *Dissertation Abstracts International* 47: 1183A.

Burns, A. 1984a. Information technology—for better or worse? In *New information technology,* ed. A. Burns, 187–215. Chichester, England: Ellis Horwood Limited.

———. 1984b. Introduction, "Knowledge is power." In *New information technology,* ed. A. Burns, 13–23. Chichester, England: Ellis Horwood Limited.

Burns, H. 1984. Recollections of first-generation computer-assisted prewriting. In *The computer in composition instruction; A writer's tool,* ed. W. Wresch. Urbana, Ill.: National Council of Teachers of English.

Burtis, P., C. Bereiter, M. Scardamalia, and J. Tetroe. 1983. The development of planning in writing. In *Explorations in the development of writing,* ed. G. Wells and B. Kroll, 153–174. Chichester, England: John Wiley.

Calkins, L. M. 1986. *The art of teaching.* Portsmouth, N.H.: Heinemann.

Candler, A. 1987. Computer aids for the handicapped. *Computers in the Schools* 3: 51–58.

Carrithers, D. 1987. Future student learning needs: A national Delphi study for high school curriculum planning. Doctoral dissertation, University of Connecticut, 1986. *Dissertation Abstracts International* 48: 01A.

Cartwright, G. P. 1988. Technology and education. Presentation at the School of Education, University of Miami.

Chaiklin, S., and M. Lewis. 1988. Will there be teachers in the classroom of the future? . . . But we don't think about that. *Teachers College Record* 89: 431–440.

Cheever, M. 1987. The effects of using a word processor on the acquisition of composition skills by the elementary student. Doctoral dissertation, Northwestern University, 1987. *Dissertation Abstracts International* 48: 43A.

Cirello, V. 1987. The effect of word processing on the writing abilities of tenth grade remedial writing students. Doctoral dissertation, New York University, 1986. *Dissertation Abstracts International* 47: 2531.

Clements, D. H., and B. K. Nastasi. 1988. Social and cognitive interactions in educational computer environments. *American Educational Research Journal* 25: 87–106.

Cohen, E., and M. Scardamalia. 1983. The effects of instructional intervention in the revision of essays by grade six children. Paper presented at the American Educational Research Association, April, Montreal.

Cohen, M., and R. Lanham. 1984. HOMER: Teaching style with a microcomputer. In *The computer in composition instruction: A writer's tool,* ed. W. Wresch, 83–90. Urbana, Ill.: National Council of Teachers of English.

Cohen, M., and M. Riel. 1986. *Computer networks: Creating real audiences for students' writing* (Report No. 15). La Jolla: University of California at San Diego.

Collier, R. M. 1983. The word processor and revision strategies. *College Composition and Communication* 34: 149–155.

Collins, A. 1983. *Learning to read and write with personal computers.* Reading Education Report No. 42. Champaign: University of Illinois at Urbana-Champaign, Center for the Study of Reading.

Collins, A., and D. Gentner. 1980. A framework for a cognitive theory of writing. In *Cognitive processes in writing,* ed. L. Gregg and E. Steinberg, 51–72. Hillsdale, N.J.: Lawrence Erlbaum Associates.

Collins, T. 1986. Micros for LD college writers: Rewriting documentation for word-processing programs. *Learning Disabilities Focus* 2: 49–54.

Collis, K. 1987. Levels of reasoning and the assessment of mathematics performance. In *The monitoring of school mathematics: Background papers: Vol. 2,* ed. T. Romberg and D. Stewart, 203–224. Madison: Wisconsin Center for Education Research.

∨ Culbertson, J. A. 1986. Whither computer literacy? In *Microcomputers and education,* ed. J.S. Culbertson and L. L. Cunningham, 109–131. Chicago: National Society for the Study of Education.

Culbertson, J. A., and L. L. Cunningham, 1986. Preface. In *Microcomputers and education,* ed. J. S. Culbertson and L. L. Cunningham, ix–x. Chicago: National Society for the Study of Education.

Curtiss, D. 1984. The experience of composition and word processing: An ethnographic, phenomenological study of high school seniors. Doctoral dissertation, Boston University, 1984. *Dissertation Abstracts International* 45: 1021.

Daiute, C. 1983. The computer as stylus and audience. *College Composition and Communication* 34: 134–145.

_____. 1985a. Do writers talk to themselves? In *The acquisition of written language: Response and revision,* ed. S. Freedman, 133–159. Norwood, N.J.: Ablex.

_____. 1985b. *Writing and computers.* Reading, Mass.: Addison-Wesley.

_____. 1986. Physical and cognitive factors in revising: Insights from studies with computers. *Research in the Teaching of English* 20: 141–159.

Dalton, D., and M. Hannafin. 1987. The effects of word processing on written composition. *Journal of Educational Research* 80: 339–342.

Dalton, D., and J. Watson. 1986. Word processing and the writing process: Enhancement or distraction? Paper presented at the Annual Convention of the Association for Educational Communications and Technology, Las Vegas.

Davies, I. K., and H. G. Shane. 1986. Educational implications of microelectronic networks. In *Microcomputers and education: Eighty-fifth yearbook of the National Society for the Study of Education,* ed. J. Culbertson and L. Cunningham, 1–21. Chicago: University of Chicago Press.

Dickinson, D. 1986. Cooperation, collaboration, and a computer: Integrating a computer into a first-second grade writing program. *Research in the Teaching of English* 20: 357–378.

Dunn, S., S. Florio-Ruane, and C. Clark. 1985. The teacher as respondent to the high school writer. In *The acquisition of written language: Response and revision,* ed. S. Freedman, 33–50. Norwood, N.J.: Ablex.

Education for All Handicapped Children Act. 1975. Public Law 94-142. Ninety-fourth Congress, November 29.

Epstein, J. 1986. The computer as a cure for writing pains. *Perspectives for Teachers of the Hearing Impaired* 4: 2–5.

Faigley, L., R. Cherry, D. Jolliffe, and A. Skinner. 1985. *Assessing writers' knowledge and processes of composing.* Norwood, N.J.: Ablex Publishing.

Fernandez, M. 1988. The influence of word processing on the written revision practices of sixth-grade students. Doctoral dissertation, Rutgers University, 1987. *Dissertation Abstracts International* 48: 3040A.

Fitzgerald, J. 1987. Research on revision in writing. *Review of Educational Research* 57: 481–506.

Flavell, J. 1985. *Cognitive development,* 2d ed. Englewood Cliffs, N.J.: Prentice-Hall.

Flower, L., and J. Hayes. 1980. The dynamics of composing: Making plans and juggling constraints. In *Cognitive processes in writing,* ed. L. W. Gregg and E. R. Steinberg, 31–50. Hillsdale, N.J.: Lawrence Erlbaum Associates.

———. 1986. Writing research and the writer. *American Psychologist* 41: 1106–1113.

Gere, A. 1986. Teaching writing: The major theories. In *The teaching of writing*, ed. A. Petrosky and D. Bartholomae, 30–48. Chicago: National Society for the Study of Education.

———. 1987. *Writing groups: History, theory, and implications.* Carbondale: Southern Illinois University Press.

Gerlach, G. 1987. The effect of typing skill on using a word processor for composition. ERIC Document Reproduction Service No. ED 286 465.

Gibbon, S. 1983. The electronic learning environment of the future. In *The future of electronic learning*, ed. M. A. White. Hillsdale, N.J.: Lawrence Erlbaum Associates.

Goldman, S., and J. Pellegrino. 1987. Information processing and educational microcomputing: Where do we go from here? *Journal of Learning Disabilities* 20: 144–154.

Goldman, S., and R. Rueda. 1988. Developing writing skills in bilingual exceptional children. *Exceptional Children* 54: 543–551.

Goodspeed, J. 1988. Two million microcomputers now used in U.S. Schools. *Electronic Learning* 7: 16–17.

Graham, S., and K. Harris. 1988. Research and instruction in written language: Introduction to the special issue. *Exceptional Children* 54: 495–496.

Graham, S., and C. MacArthur. 1988. Improving learning disabled students' skills at revising essays produced on a word processor: Self-instructional strategy training. *Journal of Special Education* 22: 133–152.

Graves, D. 1983. *Writing: Teachers and children at work.* Portsmouth, N.H.: Heinemann.

————. 1984. *A researcher learns to write*. Exeter, N.H.: Heinemann.

Graves, D., and J. Hansen. 1983. The author's chair. *Language Arts* 60: 176–183.

Haas, C. 1988. How word processing affects planning in writing: The impact of technology. Paper presented at the American Educational Research Association, New Orleans.

Haas, C., and J. R. Hayes. 1986. What did I just say? Reading problems in writing with a machine. *Research in the Teaching of English* 20: 22–35.

Hammill, D., and S. Larsen. 1978. *The test of written language*. Austin: Pro-Ed.

Harris, K., and S. Graham. 1988. Instructional recommendations for teaching writing to exceptional students. *Exceptional Children* 54: 506–512.

Harris, J. 1985. Student writers and word processors: A preliminary evaluation. *College Composition and Communication* 36: 323–330.

Hawkins, J., and K. Sheingold. 1986. The beginning of a story: Computers and the organization of learning in classrooms. In *Microcomputers and education: Eighty-fifth yearbook of the National Society for the Study of Education,* ed. J. Culbertson and J. Cunningham, 40–58. Chicago: University of Chicago Press.

Hayes, J., and L. Flower. 1980. Identifying the organization of the writing process. In *Cognitive processes in writing,* ed. L. W. Gregg and E. R. Steinberg, 3–39. Hillsdale, N.J.: Lawrence Erlbaum Associates.

————. 1983. Uncovering cognitive processes in writing: An introduction to protocol analysis. In *Research on writing:*

Principles and methods, ed. P. Mosenthal, L. Tamor, and S. Walmsley, 207–220. New York: Longman.

Heap, J. 1986. Collaborative practices during computer writing in a first grade classroom. Paper presented at the American Educational Research Association, San Francisco.

Heath, S. B., and A. Branscombe. 1985. "Intelligent writing" in an audience community: Teacher, students, and researcher. In *The acquisition of written language: Response and revision,* ed. S. Freedman, 3–32. Norwood, N.J.: Ablex.

Henney, M. 1988. Fifth and sixth graders use the Story Tree software to write stories for second and third graders. Unpublished manuscript, Iowa State University, Ames.

Hillocks, G. 1986. The writer's knowledge: Theory, research, and implications for practice. In *The teaching of writing: Eighty-fifth yearbook of the National Society for the Study of Education: Part II,* ed. A. Petrosky and D. Bartholomae, 71–94. Chicago: University of Chicago Press.

Hoffman, R. 1983. *Microcomputers and teachers.* Denver: Love Publishing.

Huffman, D., and J. Goldberg. 1987. Using word processing to teach ESL composition. *System* 15: 169–175.

Jacobi, C. 1986. Word processing for special needs students: Is there really a gain? *Educational Technology* 26: 36–39.

Johnson, D. L. 1986. Selecting a computer for your special education classroom. *Computers in the Schools* 3: 21–28.

Kaplan, H. 1986. Computers and composition: Improving students' written performance. Doctoral dissertation, University of Massachusetts, 1986. *Dissertation Abstracts International* 47: 776A.

Kerchner, L., and B. Kistinger. 1984. Language processing/word processing: Written expression, computers and learning disabled students. *Learning Disability Quarterly* 7: 329–335.

Kiefer, K. 1987. Revising on a word processor: What's happened, What's ahead? *ADE Bulletin* 87: 24–27.

Kiefer, K., and C. Smith. 1984. Improving students' revising and editing: The Writer's Workbench. In *The computer in composition instruction: A writer's tool,* ed. W. Wresch, 65–82. Urbana, Ill.: National Council of Teachers of English.

Kinkead, J. 1987. Computer conversations: E-mail and writing instruction. *College Composition and Communication* 38: 337–341.

Knapp, L. R. 1986. *The word processor and the writing teacher.* Englewood Cliffs, N.J.: Prentice-Hall.

Kolligian, J., and R. Sternberg. 1987. Intelligence, information processing, and specific learning disabilities: A triarchic synthesis. *Journal of Learning Disabilities* 20: 8–17.

Kurth, R. 1987. Word processing and composition revision strategies. ERIC Document Reproduction Service No. ED 283 195.

Kurth, R., and L. Kurth. 1987. A comparison of writing instruction using word processing, word processing with voice synthesis, and no word processing in kindergarten and first grade. Paper presented at the annual meeting of the American Educational Research Association, Washington, D.C.

Kurth, R., and L. Stromberg. 1984. Using word processing in composition instruction. Paper presented at the American Reading Forum, Sarasota, Fla.

Lansing, M. 1984. Student writers and word processors: A case study. ERIC Document Reproduction Service No. ED 249 491.

Lederer, J. 1985. Writing is FUNdamental: Composition and word processing curriculum. ERIC Document Reproduction Service No. ED 258 426.

Lehrer, R., B. Levin, P. DeHart, and M. Comeaux. 1987. Voice-feedback as a scaffold for writing: A comparative study. *Educational Computing Research* 3: 335–353.

Levin, J. A., M. J. Boruta, and M. T. Vasconcellos. 1983. Microcomputer-based environments for writing. In *Classroom computers and cognitive science,* ed. A. C. Wilkinson, 219–232. New York: Academic Press.

Levin, J. A., M. M. Riel, R. D. Rowe, and M. J. Boruta. 1985. Muktuk meets jacuzzi: Computer networks and elementary school writers. In *The acquisition of written language: Response and revision,* ed. S. Freedman, 160–171. Norwood, N.J.: Ablex.

Loheyde, K. M. 1984. Computer use in the teaching of composition: Considerations for teachers of writing. *Computers in the Schools* 1: 81–85.

Lytle, M. 1988. Word processors and writing: The relation of seventh grade students' learner characteristics and revision behaviors. Doctoral dissertation, University of Oregon, 1987. *Dissertation Abstracts International* 48: 2852.

MacArthur, C. A. 1988. The impact of computers on the writing process. *Exceptional Children* 54: 536–542.

MacArthur, C. A., and S. Graham. 1987. Learning disabled students' composing under three methods of text production: Handwriting, word processing, and dictation. *Journal of Special Education* 21: 22–42.

MacArthur, C. A., and B. Shneiderman. 1986. Learning disabled students' difficulties in learning to use a word processor: Implications for instruction and software evaluation. *Journal of Learning Disabilities* 19: 193–256.

Macrorie, K. 1980. *Searching writing.* New York: Hayden Books.

Maddux, C. D. 1984. Breaking the Everest syndrome in educational computing: An interview with Gregory Jackson and Judah L. Schwartz. *Computers in the Schools* 1: 37–48.

Madian, J. 1986. New flexibility in curriculum development through word processing. *Educational Leadership* 43: 22–23.

Mandler, J. M., and N. S. Johnson. 1977. Remembrance of things parsed: Story structure and recall. *Cognitive Psychology* 9: 111–151.

Marcus, S. 1983. Not seeing is relieving: Invisible writing with computers. *Educational Technology* 23: 12–15.

_____. 1987. Getting on-line: Computers and writing instruction. *Community, Technical, and Junior College Journal* 58: 38–39.

McClintock, R. O. 1988. Marking the second frontier. *Teachers College Record* 89: 345–351.

McCutchen, D., and C. Perfetti. 1982. Coherence and connectedness in the development of discourse production. *Text* 2: 113–119.

Mehan, H., B. Miller-Souviney, and M. Riel. 1984. Research currents: Knowledge of text editing and control of literacy skills. *Language Arts* 61: 510–515.

Meyers, L. 1984. Unique contributions of microcomputers to language intervention with handicapped children. *Seminars in Speech and Language* 5, 23–34.

Michie, D. 1986. *On machine intelligence,* 2d ed. Chichester, England: Ellis Horwood Limited.

Miller, S. 1985. Plugging your pencil into the wall: An investigation of word processing and writing skills at the middle school level. Doctoral dissertation, University of Oregon, 1984. *Dissertation Abstracts International* 45: 3535A.

Monahan, B. 1986. The relationship between previous training in computer science and the acquisition of word processing skills. *Educational Technology* 26: 22–25.

Moore, M. 1987. The effect of word processing technology in a developmental writing program on writing quality, attitude towards composing, and revision strategies of fourth and fifth grade students. Doctoral dissertation, University of South Florida, 1987. *Dissertation Abstracts International* 48: 635A.

Morocco, C., and S. Neuman. 1986. Word processors and the acquisition of writing strategies. *Journal of Learning Disabilities* 19: 243–247.

Nash, J., and L. Schwartz. 1987. Computers and the writing process. *Collegiate Microcomputer* 5: 45–48.

National Council of Teachers of English. 1983. *Guidelines for Review and Evaluation of English Language Arts Software.* Urbana, Ill.: National Council of Teachers of English.

Neuwirth, C. 1984. Toward the design of a flexible, computer-based writing environment. In *The computer in composition instruction: A writer's tool,* ed. W. Wresch, 191–204. Urbana, Ill.: National Council of Teachers of English.

Newell, A., and H. Simon. 1972. *Human problem solving.* Englewood Cliffs, N.J.: Lawrence Erlbaum Associates.

New products. 1988. *Electronic Learning* (May–June): 76, 78, 80.

Nix, D. 1988. Should computers know what you can do with them? *Teachers College Record* 89: 418–430.

Nora, S., and A. Minc. 1980. *The computerization of society: A report to the president of France.* Cambridge, Mass.: MIT Press.

Paisley, W., and M. Chen. 1982. Children and electronic text: Challenges and opportunities of the "new literacy." NIE study, Institute for Communication Research.

Papert, S. 1980. *Mindstorms.* New York: Basic Books.

Patterson, J. H. and M. S. Smith. 1986. The role of computers in higher-order thinking. In *Microcomputers and education: Eighty-fifth yearbook of the National Society for the Study of Education,* ed. J. Culbertson and J. Cunningham, 81–108. Chicago: University of Chicago Press.

Pea, R. D., and D. M. Kurland. 1987. Cognitive technologies in writing. *Review of Research in Education* 14: 277–326.

Pearson, H., and A. Wilkinson. 1986. The use of the word processor in assisting children's writing development. *Educational Review* 38: 169–187.

Pernia, S. 1988. Effects of microcomputer use and word processing on the writing skills of learning disabled middle school students. Doctoral dissertation, The University of Michigan, 1987. *Dissertation Abstracts International* 48: 2799.

Phenix, J., and E. Hannan. 1984. Word processing in the grade one classroom. *Language Arts* 61: 804–812.

Piper, A. 1987. Helping learners to write: A role for the word processor. *ELT Journal* 41: 119–125.

Piper-McGraw, K. 1983. Separating wheat from chaff: Evaluating word processing programs for language arts instruction. *Computers, Reading, and Language Arts* 1: 9–14.

Pivarnik, B. 1986. The effect of training in word processing on the writing quality of eleventh grade students. Doctoral dissertation, University of Connecticut, 1985. *Dissertation Abstracts International* 46: 1827.

Profetto, L. 1987. Investigation of attitudinal change toward informational writing using AT&T's "Writer's Workbench." Doctoral dissertation, Illinois State University, 1987. *Dissertation Abstracts International* 48: 907.

Provenzo, E. 1986. *Beyond the Gutenberg galaxy: Microcomputers and the emergence of the post-typographic culture.* New York: Teachers College Press.

Reid, T. 1986. Writing with microcomputers in a fourth grade classroom: An ethnographic study. Doctoral dissertation, Washington State University, 1985. *Dissertation Abstracts International* 47: 817A.

Rensberger, B. 1988. New Computer works 1,000 times faster. *The Washington Post* (March 14); pp. 1, 16.

Rentel, V., and M. King. 1983. Present at the beginning. In *Research on writing: Principles and methods,* ed. P. Mosenthal, L. Tamor, and S. Walmsley, 139–176. New York: Longman.

Riel, M. 1983. Education and ecstasy: Computer chronicles of students writing together. *Quarterly Newsletter of the Laboratory of Comparative Human Cognition* 3: 59–67.

Roblyer, M., W. Castine, and F. King. 1988. Assessing the impact of computer-based instruction: A review of recent research. *Computers in the Schools* 5: 1–149 (special issue).

Rodrigues, D., and R. Rodrigues. 1986. *Teaching writing with a word processor, grades 7–13.* Urbana, Ill.: National Council of Teachers of English.

Rosegrant, T. 1986. It doesn't sound right: The role of speech output as a primary form of feedback for beginning text revision. Paper presented at the annual meeting of the American Educational Research Association, San Francisco.

Rosegrant, T., and R. Cooper. 1983. *The talking screen textwriter.* Phoenix: Computing Adventures.

Rosenbaum, N. 1984. Problems with current research in writing using the microcomputer. Paper presented at the Spring Conference of the Delaware Valley Writing Council, Villanova, Pa.

Rubin, A. 1983. The computer confronts language arts: Cans and shoulds for education. In *Classroom computers and cognitive science,* ed. A. C. Wilkinson, 201–217. New York: Academic Press.

Rubin, A., and B. Bruce. (1984). *QUILL: Reading and writing with a microcomputer.* Reading Research Report No. 48. Champaign: University of Illinois at Urbana-Champaign, Center for the Study of Reading.

———. 1985. QUILL: Reading and writing with a microcomputer. In *Advances in reading/language research,* ed. B. A. Hutton, Vol. 3,97–117. Greenwich, Conn.: JAI Press.

Scardamalia, M., and C. Bereiter. 1982. Assimilative processes in composition planning. *Educational Psychologist* 17: 165–171.

_____. 1983. The development of evaluative, diagnostic, and remedial capabilities in children's composing. In *The psychology of written language: Developmental and educational perspectives*, ed. M. Martlew, 67–95. London: John Wiley.

_____. 1985. The development of dialectical processes in writing. In *Literacy, language, and learning: The nature and consequences of reading and writing*, ed. D. Olsen, N. Torrance, and A. Hildyard, 307–329. Cambridge, England: Cambridge University Press.

_____. 1986. Research on written composition. In *Handbook of research on teaching*, ed. M. Wittrock, 3d, ed., 778–803. New York: Macmillan.

Scardamalia, M., C. Bereiter, and H. Goelman. 1982. The role of production factors in writing ability. In *What writers know: The language, process, and structure of written discourse*, ed. M. Nystrand, 173–210. New York: Academic Press.

Schanck, E. 1986. Word processor versus "the pencil" effects on writing. ERIC Document Reproduction Service No. ED 270 791.

Schwartz, H. 1984. Teaching writing with computer aids. *College English* 46: 239–247.

Selfe, C. 1984. Wordsworth II: Process-based CAI for college. In *The computer in composition instruction: A writer's tool*, ed. W. Wresch, 174–190. Urbana, Ill.: National Council of Teachers of English.

Sharples, M. 1985. *Cognition, computers, and creative writing.* Chichester, England: Ellis Horwood Limited.

Shinn, J. 1987. The effectiveness of word processing and problem solving computer use on the skills of learning disabled students. Doctoral dissertation, United States International University, 1986. *Dissertation Abstracts International* 47: 4069.

Sinatra, R. 1987. Semantic networking and reading and writing effectiveness. *NYC Challenge: Journal of the New York City Association for Supervision and Curriculum Development* 2: 32–36.

Smith, F. 1982. *Writing and the writer.* New York: Holt, Rinehart and Winston.

Soled, S., B. Schare, H. Clark, S. Dunn, and B. Gilman.1989. The effects of using interactive video on cognitive achievement and attitude toward learning. Paper presented at the annual meeting of the American Educational Research Association, San Francisco, Cal.

Solomon, C. 1986. *Computer environments for children.* Cambridge, Mass.: MIT Press.

Sommers, E. 1984. What research tells us about composing and computing. Paper presented to the Computer Educators League, Buffalo, N.Y.

Stein, N., and G. Glenn. 1979. An analysis of story comprehension in elementary school children. In *New directions in discourse processing,* ed. R. Freedle, Vol. 2, 53–120. Norwood, N.J.: Ablex.

Sternberg, R. J. 1985. *Beyond IQ: A triarchic theory of human intelligence.* New York: Cambridge University Press.

Stroble, E. 1988. A look at writers' comments shared on computer screens: Can electronic mail facilitate peer group response?

Paper presented at the annual meeting of the American Educational Research Association, New Orleans.

Stromberg, L., and R. Kurth. 1983. Using word processing to teach revision in written composition. Paper presented at the National Reading Conference, Austin.

Swanson, H. L. 1987. Information processing theory and learning disabilities: An overview. *Journal of Learning Disabilities* 20: 3–7.

Sweeney, J. 1986. Comparison of the effects of three instructional delivery modes on the writing performance of eighth graders (microcomputer, methods, composition process). Doctoral dissertation, Boston University, 1986. *Dissertation Abstracts International* 47: 1595.

Tamor, L., and J. T. Bond. 1983. Text analysis: Inferring process from product. In *Research on writing: Principles and methods,* ed. P. Mosenthal, L. Tamor, and S. Walmsley, 99–138. New York: Longman.

Thomas, I. 1985. *Uses of the computer in teaching the composing process: 1985 annual report of the NCTE Committee on Instructional Technology,* Philadelphia: National Council of Teachers of English.

Thompson, D. 1987. Teaching writing on a local area network. *Technological Horizons in Education* 15: 92–97.

Toffler, A. 1974. *Future shock.* New York: Bantam.

Van Allen, R. 1976. *Language experience in communication.* Boston: Houghton Mifflin.

Von Blum, R., and M. Cohen. 1984. WANDAH: Writing-Aid and Author's Helper. In *The computer in composition instruction: A writer's tool,* ed. W. Wresch, 154–173. Urbana, Ill.: National Council of Teachers of English.

Walker, D. F. 1986. Computers and the curriculum. In *Microcomputers and education: Eighty-fifth yearbook of the National Society for the Study of Education,* ed. J. Culbertson and J. Cunningham, 22–39. Chicago: University of Chicago Press.

Weizenbaum, J. 1984. Another view from MIT. *BYTE: The Small Systems Journal* 9: 225.

Wiburg, K. 1988. The effect of different computer-based learning environments on fourth grade students' cognitive abilities. Doctoral dissertation, United States International University, 1987. *Dissertation Abstracts International* 48: 2853A.

Wilkinson, A. C., and J. Patterson. 1983. Issues at the interface of theory and practice. In *Classroom computers and cognitive science,* ed. A. C. Wilkinson, 1–13. New York: Academic Press.

Womble, G. 1984. Process and processor: Is there room for a machine in the English classroom? *English Journal* 73: 34–37.

Woolley, W. 1986. The effects of word processing on the writing of selected fifth-grade students. Doctoral dissertation, College of William and Mary, 1985. *Dissertation Abstracts International* 47: 82A.

Wresch, W. (ed.). 1984a. *The computer in composition instruction.* Urbana, Ill.: National Council of Teachers of English.

———. 1984b. Questions, answers, and automated writing. In *The computer in composition instruction: A writer's tool,* ed. W. Wresch, 143–153. Urbana, Ill.: National Council of Teachers of English.

Young, J. 1984. Videodisc simulation: Tomorrow's technology today. *Computers in the Schools* 1: 49–58.

Adaptations, educational: for hearing impaired students, 115–116; for learning disabled students, 109–111; for linguistically different students, 116–118; for physically handicapped students, 112–113; for visually impaired students, 113–115

Adaptive devices: for oral communication, 112–113; for written expression, 112–115

Adolescents: academic expectations for, 83; cognitive characteristics of, 91; writing process development for, 85

AI. See Artificial intelligence (AI)

Ammon, P., 32

Anderson, D., 103

Anderson, J. R., 11, 12, 26, 30, 36

Anderson, R., 23

Applebee, A., 36, 38, 43, 62, 74, 84, 86

Artificial intelligence (AI): and computer-assisted instruction, 19; fear of, 8; and knowledge construction, 13; impact on education, 3; and information processing, 9–13; and natural language understanding, 146; as a paradigm for composition, 36; and theory construction, 9

Automaticity: defined, 30; and editing, 97; of writing processes, 31

Barraga, N., 113

Batey, A., 131

Beal, C., 68, 71

Beaugrande, R. de, 34, 36

Behrmann, M., 103

Bereiter, C., 27, 28, 31, 62, 64, 65, 66, 67, 73, 75, 76, 77, 79, 85, 86, 93, 95, 96

Biggs, J. B., 29

Bigley, A., 88, 90

Bilingual Education Act (P.L. 98–511), 101

Bloom, L., 31

Bond, J. T., 30, 33

Boone, R., 71

Borgh, K., 72

Bork, A. 16, 17, 130, 141, 145, 146, 147, 150

Boruta, M. J., 21, 56

Bos, C. S., 43

Bracewell, R. J., 28, 31

Brady, M., 116

Bramer, M., 13

Branscombe, A., 41

Bridwell, L., 48

Brisk, M., 118

Brooke, R., 48

Broudy, H. S., 7, 16
Brown, A., 23
Bruce, B., 56, 71, 74, 77, 81
Bryson, M., 88
Burnett, J., 70
Burtis, P., 86
Burns, A., 7, 8, 15, 16
Burns, H., 94

CAC. See Computer-assisted
composing (CAC)
Calkins, L., 40, 74, 79
Candler, A., 112, 114
Carrithers, D., 141
Cartwright, P., 141
Castine, W., 46, 69
CATCH Program: and knowledge
telling, 74; prompts for
elementary children, 71–72; as a
summarization aid, 96; support
for planning, 77; tool for revising,
52
Chaiklin, S., 18, 43
Cheever, M., 71
Chen, M., 143
Children, adolescents. See
Adolescents
Children, elementary age:
environmental adaptations for, 83;
characteristics of writing by, 85;
transition from speech to writing
by, 71
Cirello, V., 88
Clements, D. H., 42
Cognition: control processes, 96;
knowledge acquisition, 64;
knowledge recall, 64; memory
search, 64, 86–87; schema
development, 64–65
Cohen, E., 67
Cohen, M., 51, 53, 60
Cohen, R., 54
Collaboration: and scaffolding, 43;
for teaching and learning, 149;
within the computer writing
environment, 40; and writing

process instruction, 40; with
young children, 78–79
Collier, R. M., 48
Collins, A., 34, 77
Collins, T., 110
Collis, K. F., 29
Communication, changing nature of,
143. See also Electronic Mail
(E-Mail); Networks, computer
Composing: for elementary students,
62–67; and knowledge-telling
strategy, 64–65, 73; models of,
24–37, as problem solving, 67;
problem-solving activities for, 34;
procedural knowledge for, 66–67;
processes, 92; for secondary
students, 83–87; strategies for, 63,
65, 73, 95; substantive knowledge
for 66. See also Computer-assisted
Composing (CAC); Writing
Computer Chronicle Newswire, 78,
80
Computer-assisted composing
(CAC): to aid transition from
speech to writing, 72; attitudes of
elementary students toward, 71;
attitudes of secondary students
toward, 90; advantages of, 41; for
cognitive process enhancement,
91–97; and collaborative writing,
70; effectiveness of, 70; effects on
revision, 71; effects on
student-teacher interaction, 70;
and electronic writing supports,
56–60; for elementary students,
72–79; and fluency, 46; for
hearing impaired students,
115–116; instructional
recommendations for using, 46;
and interactive software programs,
51–56; introducing students to, 79;
knowledge needed to use,
109–110; and learning disabilities,
106–109; for learning disabled
students, 105–106; levels of
involvement for students,
121–122; for linguistically

different students, 116–118; and metacognitive process enhancement, 91–97; and networks, 59–60; for physically disabled students, 112–113; for planning, 51–56; for production, 52–56; prompting programs used with, 76–77; and quality of writing, 46, 69–72; research concerns, 60; for revising, 52–56; for secondary students, 87–90; and spelling checkers, 49–50; and style checkers, 50–51; to support knowledge construction, 67; using genre-based programs, 57–58; validation of, 67–72; for visually impaired students, 113–115; and voice synthesis, 59, 72; and writing process instruction for secondary students, 88–90; and writing strategies, 79. *See also* Composing; Word processing programs; Writing

Computer literacy, 5–6. *See also* Telematics literacy

Computers: advantages for special needs learners, 102; applications of, 19; and cognitive science, 11; communication capabilities of, 148–149; as demonstration tools, 41; as the dominant delivery system, 141; effects on society, 7–9; effects on the teaching-learning process, 19; as an expressive medium, 144; history of, 2–5; impact on learning, 7; and information lag, 16; and information processing, 10; pedagogical strengths of, 18; as a problem-solving aid, 22; stages in the development of, 2–3; used as writing tools, 22

Computer systems, components of, 124

Computer writing tools: considerations for selection of, 121–122; match to student needs,

120; need to evaluate, 119–120; phases of, 146

Computing, educational: current trends in, 141; theory of, 9, 18

Conferences: writing and computer networks, 59; goals for, 94; and improving quality of writing, 70; workshop method, 98

Cooper, R., 58

Culbertson, J. A., 2, 5, 6

Cunningham, L. L., 2

Curtiss, D., 90

Daiute, C., 4, 21, 28, 29, 41, 46, 47, 48, 52, 68, 69, 70, 71, 77, 78, 89, 96, 98, 119, 133, 135, 143

Dalton, D., 88

Databases, and report writing, 100

Davies, I. K., 2, 3, 4

Declarative knowledge: defined, 26; and the writing process, 27

Desktop publishing, and the writing process, 48

Dickinson, D., 70

Dickson, P., 116

Dickson, W., 72

Dictionaries, on-line, 49–50

DRAFT program: comment option, 55; as an integrated writing package, 55

Education for All Handicapped Children Act (P.L. 94-142), 101

Electronic Learning, 144

Electronic Mail (E-mail), conferences facilitated by, 99. *See also* Networks, computer

English as a second language (ESL), instruction in, 117

Epstein, J., 116

Environment: adaptation to, 34; for writing, 34

Environment, computer: for interactive learning, 17; quality of,

42; for elementary students,
79–81; contextual variables of,
79–80; design for, 41; for
functional learning, 44–46, 80;
future trends, 148–149; impact on
attitude, 81; impact on writing
performance, 81; interactive
nature of, 80; physical
arrangement of, 43; for secondary
students, 98–100; teacher roles
within, 43; variations in, 44;
interactive nature of, 17
Expert systems. See Artificial
intelligence

Faigley, L., 24, 28, 29, 34, 36
Feedback, through collaborative
writing, 97
Fernandez, M., 71
Fitzgerald, J., 46
Flavell, J., 28, 63
Flower, L., 28, 34, 35, 62

Gibbon, S., 148
Goals: instructional, 122; for
writing, 93, 123–124
Goelman, H., 64
Goodspeed, J., 2
Genre templates, for prose and
verse, 94
Gentner, D., 34
Gere, A., 34, 59
Gerlach, G., 68
Glenn, G., 27, 75
Goldberg, J., 117
Goldman, S., 21, 106
Graham, S., 46, 106, 108, 109
Graves, D., 17, 32, 40, 41, 47, 62,
77, 79, 81, 143
Griffin, E., 68, 71

Haas, C., 48, 49, 86
Hammill, D., 108
Hannafin, M., 88

Hannan, E., 70
Hansen, J., 40
Hardware: cost factors, 125, 128;
future trends, 144–145; selection
of, 124–128; software support
capabilities, 125
Harris, J., 46
Harris, K., 106
Hawkins, J., 18, 19, 150
Hayes, J., 28, 34, 35, 48, 62
Heap, J., 71
Hearing impaired students,
computer-assisted composing
curricula for, 116
Hearing impairments, defined, 115
Heath, S. B., 41
Henney, M., 81
Hillocks, G., 27, 28
Hoffman, R., 102
HOMER program, for textual
analysis, 51
Huffman, D., 117

Information processing: Anderson's
theory of, 11; and artificial
intelligence, 9–13; Sternberg's
theory of, 28, 33–34; system
components, 10
Integrated software programs:
evaluation of, 137; for planning,
93
Interactive programs, and
composing, 51–56

Jackson, G., 142
Jacobi, C., 107
Johnson, D. L., 124
Johnson, N. S., 27, 75

Kaplan, H., 71
Keyboard: adaptations for, 112–113;
optional input devices for, 47
Keyboard skills: acquisition of for
elementary students, 68–69;

instruction in, 46–47; learning to
use, 69; need for, 89; tutorials for
teaching, 69
Keyboard tutorials, advantages of,
92, evaluation of, 134–135
Kerchner, L., 107, 108
Kiefer, K., 97
King, F., 46, 69
King, M., 27
Kinkead, J., 99
Kistinger, B., 107, 108
Knapp, L. R., 130, 131, 134
Knowledge-telling strategy:
characteristics of, 73; model of
the, 65; steps in, 73
Knowledge-transformation strategy,
development of, 95
Kolligian, J., 28
Kurland, D. M., 123, 144
Kurth, L., 59, 68, 72
Kurth, R., 59, 68, 72, 88, 90
Kurzweil Reading Machine, 114–115

Lahey, M., 31
Langer, J., 62, 84
Language, pragmatics of: defined,
75; development of, 75; for
writing, 75
Lanham, R., 51
Lansing, M., 89
Larsen, S., 108
Learning, developmental framework
for, 29
Learning disabilities: defined, 104;
writing and, 104–105; cognitive
characteristics of, 104
Learning disabled students:
cognitive characteristics of, 104;
and instructional strategies for
writing, 110–111
Learning strategies: elementary
level, 72–76; secondary level,
91–97
Least restrictive environment,
mandate of P.L. 94–142, 102
Lederer, J., 116

Lehrer, R., 59, 72, 75
Levin, J. A., 21, 44, 56, 59, 78, 149
Lewis, M., 18, 43
Limited English Proficient (LEP):
designation as, 102; advantages of
computer assisted composing for,
117
Loheyde, K. M., 46
Lytle, M., 88, 89

MacArthur, C. A., 40, 46, 47, 60,
103, 108, 109, 119, 132, 134
McClintock, R. O., 20
Macrorie, K., 100
McCutchen, D., 64, 76
Maddux, C. D., 142
Madian, J., 81
Mainstreaming, and least restrictive
environment, 102
Mandler, J. M., 27, 75
Marcus, S., 53, 121, 129
MECC Writer program, for text
analysis, 51
Mehan, H., 80
Metacognition: and automaticity of
processes, 32; deficits in, 28;
defined, 23; development of, 63;
and metacomponents, 28; and
pragmatics of language, 75; and
text production processes, 32; and
writing ability 29; and strategy
instruction, 107, 108–109;
supports for development of, 97;
and writing deficits, 106; and
writing development, 28
Meyers, L., 111
Michie, D., 9, 11, 13, 14
Miller, S., 69
Miller-Souviney, B., 80
Minc, A., 3, 6, 142, 143
Modem, for data transmission, 124
Monahan, B., 89
Monitoring, *See* Metacognition
Moore, M., 70, 71
Morocco, C., 105, 106, 107, 109,
110

Motivation, role in writing, 31–32
Mullis, I., 62, 84
Multimedia instruction, design of, 147

NAEP, *See* National Assessment of Educational Progress
Nash, J., 98
Nastasi, B. K., 42
National Assessment of Educational Progress (NAEP), results, 62, 84, 86
National Council of Teachers of English (NCTE), Committee on Instructional Technology, 39, 127–128
Networks: for conferences, 59–60; and electronic mail, 59–60; local, 59; *See also* Networks, computer
Networks, computer: communication options, 112; Computer Chronicle Newswire, 78, 80; and E-mail, 99; and hearing impaired students, 116; national, 3; subscriptions to, 3–4; for three-way interaction, 123; uses of, 3–4; use within a functional writing environment, 45. *See also* Conferences; Electronic mail (E-mail); Networks; Telematics
Network systems, evaluation of, 135
Neumann, S., 105, 106, 107, 109, 110
Neuwirth, C., 55
Newell, A., 36
Nix, D., 19
Nora, S., 3, 6, 142, 143

Outlining: and composition, 51–55; and goal development, 93

Paisley, W., 143
Papert, S., 7, 16, 17, 19, 112

Patterson, J. H., 19, 20, 22, 42
Pea, R. D., 123, 144, 146
Pearson, H., 89
Pellegrino, J., 106
Perfetti, C., 64, 76
Performance, types of, 33
Pernia, S., 107
Phenix, J., 70
Physical disabilities: defined, 112; writing and, 111–113
Piper, A., 117, 120, 131
Piper-McGraw, K., 139
Pivarnik, B., 88
Planning: activities for, 74; as a central writing process, 20; defined, 35; instruction in, 86; and NAEP results, 86; processes, 93–95; sentence level, 48; software for, 74, 93; techniques to foster, 76–77
Print, enlargement of, 114
Printers: and desk-top publishing, 128; selection of, 128
Printing: of documents, 132; *What you see is what you get* feature, 132
Problem solving: and writing ability, 34–36; intellectual attributes of, 26
Procedural facilitation, for planning, 93
Procedural knowledge: defined, 26; and the writing process, 27
Production processes, 95–96
Profetto, L., 90
Prompting: assisted monologues for, 93–94; revision programs using, 97; software, 94
Prompting programs, evaluation of, 136
Provenzo, E., 3, 5, 6, 7

QUILL program: components of, 56; goals for, 56; as an integrated writing package, 55; and knowledge telling, 74; Planner subprogram 77; prompts for elementary students, 71; Publisher subprogram, 81

Reid, T., 80
Rensberger, B., 13
Rentel, V., 27
Report writing, methods for teaching, 100
Revision: content level, 46–96; patterns of secondary students, 89–90; processes, 96–97; prompting programs for, 52, 89–90; strategies to facilitate, 79; surface level, 46, 96
Ricketts, D., 131
Riel, M., 60, 70, 80
Roblyer, M., 46, 69
Rodrigues, D., 98, 99, 100
Rodrigues, R., 98, 99, 100
Rosegrant, T., 58, 59, 72
Rosenbaum, N., 97
Rubin, A., 22, 55, 56, 71, 74, 77, 81
Rueda, R., 21

Scaffolds: for instruction, 36–37; computers as, 74–75; voice synthesis as, 72; and writing development, 66
Scardamalia, M., 27, 28, 31, 62, 64, 65, 66, 67, 73, 75, 76, 77, 79, 85, 86, 93, 95, 96
Schank, E., 71
Schema, story: development of, 27–28; and narrative writing, 27
Schwartz, H., 99
Schwartz, J., 142
Schwartz, L., 98
SEEN program, networking for, 99
Selfe, C., 57
Sensory impairments, writing and, 111–116
Shane, H. G., 2, 3, 4
Sharples, M., 146, 147
Sheingold, K., 18, 19, 150
Shinn, J., 107

Shneiderman, B., 120, 133, 134
Simon, H., 11, 36
Sinatra, R., 52
Sirc, G., 48
Smith, F., 24
Smith, M. S., 22, 19, 42
Special needs, types of, 101–104
Speech synthesis. *See* Voice synthesis
Spelling checkers: augmented word lists, 50; evaluation of, 135; introduction to, 78; personalized dictionaries, 50; uses of, 49; use with primary school children, 71
Software: categories of, 42; characteristics of, 130; future trends in 145–148; production trends for, 146; selection of, 128–137. *See also* Word processing programs
Software evaluation, committee formation for, 124; features of, 129; reasons for, 120
Soled, S., 147
Solomon, C., 42, 144
Sommers, E., 47
Stein, N., 27, 75
Sternberg, R., 28, 33
Stroble, E., 59
Stromberg, L., 90
Structure of observed learning outcome (SOLO), taxonomy, 29–30
Style revision programs, for adolescents, 97
Substantive facilitation: for production, 93; and prompting programs, 94
Supercomputers: fifth generation computer project, 13, 15; and problem solving capabilities, 13–14
Swanson, H. L., 10
Sweeney, J., 88

Tamor, L., 30, 33

Teachers: preparation programs for, 149–150; role shifts for, 19, 43

Teaching strategies: elementary level, 76–79; secondary level, 91–97

Technology; impact on education, 16; impact on society, 8–9, 16; and levels of learning, 7. *See also* Artificial intelligence (AI); Computers

Telematics: and data transmission, 142; defined, 3; impact on learning, 142; implications for education, 4. *See also* Networks, computer

Telematics literacy: defined, 6; philosophy of, 8. *See also* Computer literacy

TETRAscan II, as an adaptive communication aid, 113

Text analysis, introduction to, 78

Text analysis programs, evaluation of, 136

Text reformatting, for analysis, 123

Thesauruses, on-line, 49–50

Think Tank program, as a genre-based program, 51–52

Thinking Networks program, using semantic mapping, 52

Thomas, I., 39

Toffler, A., 4, 150

Typing. *See* Keyboard; Keyboard skills

Van Allen, R., 47

Vasconcellos, M. T., 21, 56

VersaBraille II, for word processing, 115

Videodisk simulations, support for, 147

Videodisk technology, impact on instruction, 147

Videotext, and language arts instruction, 143

Visual handicaps, defined, 113–114

Voice synthesis: and collaborative writing, 72; and composing, 58–59; and editing, 72; use with visually handicapped students, 114

Von Blum, R., 53, 54

Walker, D. F., 18

WANDAH program: commenting aid, 55; components of, 53; prewriting aids, 53; revising aids, 53–55; underlying assumptions, 53

Watson, J., 88

Weizenbaum, J., 7

Wiburg, K., 74

Wilkinson, A. C., 20, 89

Window feature: and planning, 48; uses of, 96

Wittrock, M. C., 65

Word processing: accessibility to student writing, 107; advantages, 46–49; advantages for special needs learners, 103; and ESL instruction, 117–118; and planning, 48; and revision, 46–47; and writing process instruction, 17, 70, 108

Word processing programs: adaptive devices for, 133; evaluations of, 130–134; features of, 131–134; file handling, 132; for hearing impaired students, 116; instructional decisions when using, 130–131; manual adaptations for, 110–111; and printers, 132; for procedural facilitation, 78; for elementary students, 69; for adolescents, 134; for nine- to thirteen-year-old writers, 134; for writers with special needs, 134; support features for, 133; text entry and edit features, 131–132; and text formatting, 132; and word-wrap feature, 131; for young writers, 131, 133–134. *See also* Computer-assisted composing (CAC)

Wresch, W., 41, 52, 87, 143
Womble, G., 89
Woolley, W., 69
Word wrap, as an essential feature, 131
Writer's Helper program, an integrated software package, 52–53
Writer's Workbench program, for style checking, 50
Writing: and audience awareness, 41; Beaugrande's model for, 36; cognitive framework for, 24; cognitive nature of, 23–30; cognitive perspective of, 21; deficiencies, 105–106; development of basic skills, 62–63; development of cognitive processes, 63, 85; evaluation of software for, 135; Flower and Hayes' model for, 34–36; functional-interactive perspective of, 21; intellectual attributes of, 26–30, and language development, 30–31; and learning experiences, 30–33; and natural process instruction, 28; nature of, 20–22; poor performance of, 84; as problem solving, 34–36; problem solving strategies for, 63–64; second-generation research in, 24;

as a social-communicative act, 34; software for narrative, 75; tasks and contexts for, 33–37; tools for, 42. *See also* Composing; Computer-assisted composing (CAC)
Writing instruction: goals of, 95; individualization of, 123; program needs, 125; using peer tutoring, 120
Writing processes: automaticity of, 30; and metacognition, 35; organization of, 35–36; procedural facilitation for, 78; substantive facilitation for, 78. *See also* Writing
Writing process instruction: authors' chairs, 40–41; for elementary students, 70, 76–79; features of, 40–41; and instructional scaffolds, 43; milieu for, 90; publication of student work, 81; for secondary students, 91–97; and word processing, 17, 108
Writing process software: dictionaries and thesauruses, 49–50; levels of, 49–56; integrated programs, 51–56; style checkers, 50–51

Young, J., 147